ENJOY CHINESE COOKING
by
Judy Lew

ISBN 0-9605134-1-8

Published by   First Printing September, 1980
Lew Publishing · P.O. Box 14154   Second Printing September 1982
Seattle, Washington 98114

Illustrations by Yoshiko Tsuji of Y and Company

Photographs by George Somoff

Typesetting by Typeworks   Printed in U.S.A.

TO

WILLKIE
KIMBERLEY AND PAMELA

ACKNOWLEDGEMENTS

•

Special thanks to my parents, Hing and Po Kim Ng, for providing the initial guidance in Chinese cooking, and to my grandfather, Goey Sun Chin, for instilling an invaluable sense of enjoyment for cooking.

•

I am particularly grateful to Mrs. Nam Lew, for her generous assistance in recipe development.

•

My sincere appreciation to Mr. Tomio Moriguchi, President of Uwajimaya, Inc., for providing both the opportunity and advice in connection with the preparation of this book.

•

For the expert photography and his valued friendship, I am immensely grateful to Mr. George Somoff of George Somoff Photography.

•

I wish to thank Yoshiko Tsuji, of Y and Company, for her illustrations, creative ideas, constant encouragement, and consultation.

•

And let me not forget the debt of gratitude owed to my brother, Paul Ng — and to my students — whose participation and support over the years have made all the difference. Without them, this book would not be a reality.

●

Judy Lew was born in Kwangtung, China, and came to the United States, arriving in Seattle in 1953. A graduate of the University of Washington in Home Economics, she is presently the Home Economist and Director of the Uwajimaya Cooking School. The Uwajimaya Company is the largest Asian food and gift retailer in the Northwest. Judy is well known for her cooking classes and numerous appearances on local radio and television programs, to discuss and demonstrate many of the superb recipes which she has developed.

The writing of this book was prompted by the many requests from friends and students, her interest in preserving family recipes, and the love of cooking, which was derived from her grandfather, a professional chef.

Her cooking techniques presented in this book simplify Chinese cooking, and make it enjoyable for everyone.

●

INTRODUCTION

The title of this book expresses the intent and purpose for which it was written. You will find that the key to great Chinese cooking lies in learning to enjoy yourself foremost and letting everything else follow.

This book will guide you through the simple techniques necessary for preparing the basic ingredients contained in the easy-to-follow recipes. The recipes have been developed and tested in Chinese cooking classes, along with a few personal favorites that have been handed down from family generations. Suggestions for meal planning have been reduced to a simple chart, for quick and easy reference.

The highly nutritious ingredients and quick sealing cooking methods of Chinese cooking are consistent with the emergence of a health and diet oriented society. The informal Chinese dinner is especially suited for today's life styles. Nutritious, economical and easy to prepare, Chinese food also happens to be very delicious. Thus, this book's emphasis has been placed upon the preparation of dishes used in everyday Chinese meals.

As you gain proficiency and personal confidence in Chinese cooking you will find this book helpful in adapting various recipes to your own personal tastes and experimenting with different ingredients to achieve a desired result. I encourage all my students and readers to go beyond the recipes, substitute ingredients, and — most importantly — have fun and Enjoy Chinese Cooking.

— Judy Won Lew

CONTENTS

This section provides a working knowledge of the basic cutting and cooking techniques, menu planning and helpful tips necessary in the preparation of a successful and delicious Chinese meal.

Information

PREPARATIONS

Chinese cooking, like anything else, requires proper planning and preparation. The basic equipment should be acquired as well as an acquaintance with cutting and cooking methods. Also serving and menu ideas should be considered at the outset.

BASIC EQUIPMENT

The Wok

The Chinese wok is a round or flat-bottomed pan made of heavy gauge carbon steel. It comes in various sizes, but the most functional for our purposes is the 14-inch round-bottomed wok. The round-bottomed wok is usually accompanied by a ventilated ring which serves to support the base of the wok above a gas-range burner. A flat-bottomed wok, which does not require a ring stand, sits atop an electric range, but requires some adjustments during cooking as there is direct contact with the burner, resulting in much hotter temperatures.

When using a gas range, the ring should be situated with the sides slanting downwards and the smaller opening supporting the wok. The round-bottom design of the wok directs the heat source to the center of the wok which gets hot very quickly. The heat is then conducted rapidly and evenly throughout the rest of the wok.

Gas   Electric

When using an electric range, the ring should be placed securely over the burner, with the sides slanting upwards to allow the center of the wok closer proximity to the burner.

Seasoning the wok

Scrub the wok in hot sudsy water to remove the protective oil applied when manufactured. Rinse well and dry thoroughly. Season the cleaned wok by heat and rub a small amount of peanut oil on the inside surface with a paper towel. Re-heat the wok until hot and repeat the process two more times. Your wok is now ready for use.

During the course of cooking a meal, the wok need only be cleaned with hot water, using a bristle scrub brush or a brush used for Teflon pans. When you are through using the wok, wash in sudsy water and rinse. Dry over medium heat and rub a dab of oil on the inside surface to prevent rust. Eventually, with constant use, your wok will assume a darker color on the inside which results in smooth non-stick cooking.

Never scour your wok with harsh cleansers. If rust appears, simply scrub clean and re-season. Any time the wok is used for steaming, it must be re-seasoned afterward in order to prevent foods from sticking. However, only one coating of oil is necessary for re-seasoning your wok.

Electric woks are good substitutes. They are espeically suited for entertaining or cooking at the table. Just follow the package instructions for use and care.

Wok Accessories

Accessories specially designed for wok cooking are available in any cookware store. They greatly facilitate cooking with a wok.

Cover — The size of the dome-shaped cover depends largely upon the diameter of the wok. Sometimes a 10 or 12 inch cover to a frying pan may suffice. The convenience of a cover is readily apparent when it is necessary to steam ingredients using the wok.

Cover

Curved Spatula — This utensil comes with a long handle with a wide, curved edge which fits the curved bottom of the wok. Ingredients can be more readily tossed and removed using a curved rather than straight-edged spatula.

Draining Rack — This wire semicircular rack attaches to the top of the wok. It is used in deep-frying to drain the oil from the food before removing onto a serving dish.

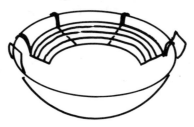

Wire Strainer — This strainer is made of wire with a long wooden handle. The large holes allow the ingredients to be removed quickly from hot oil, leaving the crumbs or bits of batter behind to be removed by a fine mesh strainer. It is also useful in removing large pieces of foods from soups or sauces.

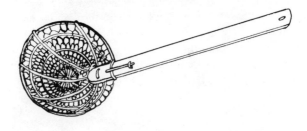

Fine Mesh Strainer — This wire utensil is used in deep-frying to remove small particles of food, thereby keeping the oil clean. It can also be used to strain bits of food from soup stock.

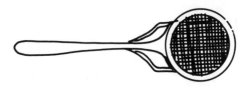

Steaming Rack — This round rack, preferably made of metal, resembles a cake rack. It is used to elevate plates of food above the boiling water in a wok while steaming. Bamboo or metal steamers with two tiers and a cover are also available, but unless a lot of food is steamed, a wok and steaming rack is sufficient.

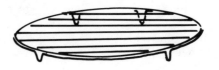

Cooking Chopsticks — These are longer than ordinary eating chopsticks. They are made of bamboo and come in various lengths. Choose the proper length by the comfort and ease of handling best suited to you.

How to use: 1) Rest the first chopstick on top of your ring finger with the thumb braced over the chopstick as shown in Diagram 1.

2) Hold the other chopstick as you would a pencil.

3) With the inside chopstick held stationary with your thumb, move the outside chopstick, forming pinchers to pick up ingredients.

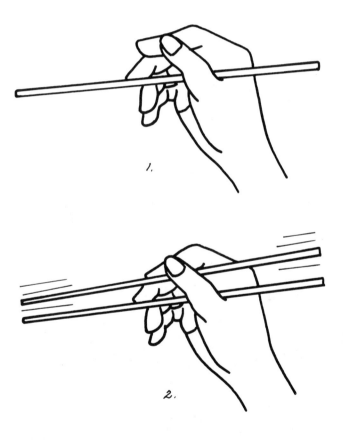

Deep-Frying Thermometer — This handy device will ensure the exact oil temperature used in recipes calling for deep-frying.

Cleaver

The basic Chinese knife is the cleaver. It is used for cutting recipe ingredients and in the same motion, transporting them to an awaiting wok or serving tray. The cleaver usually measures three to four inches wide and eight inches long. The thickness varies from thin cleavers for vegetable slicing all the way to thick bone-chopping cleavers. A sharp cleaver is necessary to perform the various cutting methods discussed in the next section. Keep your cleaver sharp by using a sharpening stone and steel as often as needed.

Rice Cooker

This is a very useful item if you cook rice often or when a large quantity of steamed rice is desired. The electric rice cooker automatically steams the rice to the proper consistency and keeps it warm until ready to serve. Rice cookers come in various capacities.

This is the basic equipment designed for Chinese cooking. Always keep in mind that alternatives in your own kitchen may work just as well. Many ordinary kitchen utensils can be adapted for use in Chinese cooking. Substitutes for the basic equipment range from a heavy frying pan in place of the traditional Chinese wok all the way to miscellaneous knives for the cleaver.

CUTTING METHODS

In Chinese cooking, all ingredients are cut into bite-size morsels before cooking or serving. This is done for aesthetic as well as functional reasons. Vegetables are more appealing with uniform slicing and chopping while ingredients cut the same size and shape cook more evenly and quickly. The following describes the various cutting techniques used in this book.

Slice — Refers to meats or vegetables cut into thin uniform strips usually two inches long by ¾ to one inch wide and about ⅛ inch thick or as directed by the recipe.

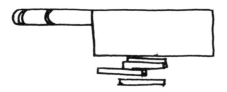

Sliver or Shred — Refers to meats or vegetables cut two inches long by ⅛ inch wide by ⅛ inch thick to resemble match-sticks or beansprouts.

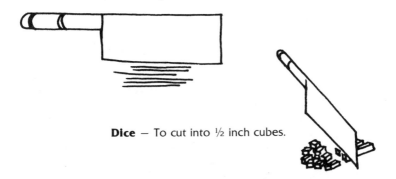

Dice — To cut into ½ inch cubes.

Chop or Mince — To cut into small pieces as in ground beef.

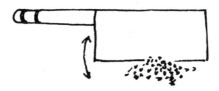

Boning a chicken

1. Place the chicken on a cutting board, breast side up. With a sharp knife, slice through the skin between the thigh and lower breast, exposing the thigh.

2. Bend the thigh back and carve around the joint to remove the thigh and leg. Remove as much meat as possible from the back of the chicken while removing the thigh and leg. Repeat with the other side in the same manner.

3. To remove meat from leg and thigh: Cut along the inside of the leg and thigh, exposing the bones. Cut the meat away from the thigh bone, separate the joint, and remove the thigh bone. Remove the rest of the meat from the leg bone. Repeat with the other leg and thigh.

4. Turn chicken over so the back is up. Cut the wings from the back to expose the joint, taking as much meat as possible from the back. Separate at the joint and pull to remove breast meat. This will leave a small piece of chicken (tenderloin) still attached to the breast bone, which should be cut out. Repeat with the other wing in the same manner.

5. Trim off as much meat from the carcass as possible. Use the bones to make soup stock.

How to bone a chicken breast

1. Place chicken breast skin side down on a cutting board. Cut ½ inch into the top of the chicken breast, breaking the white triangular piece of cartilage. Holding the chicken breast with both hands, bend it back to expose the breast bone. The bone should pop up.

2. Run thumb down the breast bone and cartilage and pull the entire bone and cartilage out.

3. Locate the wishbone at the top of the breast, which broke into two pieces when the breast was bent back. Using a sharp knife, cut as much meat from the wishbone as possible.

4. Release meat from the ribs, scraping the bones as you cut. Repeat with the other side of the chicken breast.

5. Pull skin off and cut off the fat at the bottom of the breast.

6. Remove the tendons on the underside of the breast. There is one on each side.

7. Now you have a boneless chicken breast. Use as directed in a recipe.

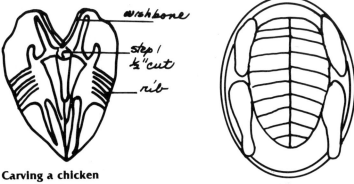

Carving a chicken

1. Remove wings, legs and thighs, set aside.

2. Separate breast from the back; set breast aside.

3. First, cut the back into bite-sized pieces (1 ½"x2") and arrange on the center of a platter.

4. Separate wings at the joints, discard tips and place wing pieces on the sides of the upper half of the platter.

5. Cut each thigh in half and place on platter. Place the legs on the sides of the lower half of the platter.

6. Cut breast into bite-sized pieces and place on top of back pieces.

7. Garnish with parsley.

This method of carving can also be used to cut a chicken in preparation for cooking.

COOKING METHODS

The most common Chinese cooking methods include stir-frying, deep-frying, roasting, and steaming. Depending upon the method utilized, ingredients generally retain their natural flavor and nutrition with new and different tastes emerging from the use of each method.

Stir-Frying

This method of cooking combines the elements of high heat and quick, constant tossing to seal in the flavor and juices of meats and vegetables. Stir-frying cooks protein foods thoroughly at the same time leaving them tender and juicy. Vegetables stir-fried until barely tender retain their natural color and crisp texture.

Only a small amount of oil is necessary. Timing and temperature will vary according to the type of pan selected and whether a gas or electric range is used. A flat-bottomed pan or wok which has contact with the heating element will get much hotter than a round-bottomed one. In addition, a gas range is more convenient since you can turn the heat up or down instantly. A good stir-frying temperature is 375 degrees Fahrenheit. If the temperature is too high, the food will burn in which case a lower temperature adjustment is in order. On the other hand, if the temperature is too low, ingredients do not fry, but seep in the oil and will lose their flavor. Therefore, to maintain the proper temperature, constant adjustment of the temperature may be necessary.

Actual stir-frying involves vigorous arm action in the constant stirring and tossing of the food. It is a loud and noisy operation when the food meets the pan and the stirring begins. Actual cooking time will seldom exceed several minutes.

(Follow the steps below for effective stir-frying:)

1) Heat the wok until it barely gets hot and add oil (usually 2 tablespoons).

2) Roll the oil around to cover the cooking surface of the wok.

3) When the oil begins to form a light haze, you are ready to add the ingredients.

4) Follow the recipe and remember to adjust the temperature control for the proper stir-frying temperature.

Cornstarch for thickening

Sauces or gravies can be thickened with a variety of starches such as arrowroot, potato, tapioca, or cornstarch. All of these starches produce a translucent gravy, whereas flour will produce an opaque gravy. In Chinese cooking, cornstarch is most often used.

Many recipes call for cornstarch for thickening, but sometimes an exact amount is not given. Mix equal amounts of cornstarch to cold water and stir until cornstarch is dissolved. Usually one tablespoon of cornstarch dissolved in one tablespoon of cold water will be enough to thicken ½ cup of sauce to produce a medium thick gravy.

To thicken a sauce, always push all ingredients to the side of the wok, making a well at the bottom of the wok. Stir cornstarch mixture and pour a small amount into the well. Stir the sauce constantly to prevent lumps. Allow the sauce to come to a boil and see how thick it is. If not thick enough, add more cornstarch mixture until desired thickness is obtained. Always remember to stir the sauce constantly to prevent lumps from forming. When desired thickness is obtained, mix ingredients together gently to coat with sauce.

Deep-Frying

Deep-frying requires a large amount of oil in the wok, usually not more than 3-4 cups. A fourteen inch wok is best suited for deep-frying. As with stir-frying, timing and temperature for deep-frying will vary depending upon whether a gas or electric stove is used. Thus, the time given for most recipes is only approximate and adjustments should be made accordingly. Added caution should be exercised whenever oil is used at high temperatures. Never leave the hot oil unattended!

The proper temperature for deep-frying is generally 375 degrees. The oil should reach this temperature before any ingredients are added. At a temperature of 375 degrees, the oil will just barely begin to smoke. An easy way to tell whether the oil has reached the desired temperature is to add a drop of batter into the oil. If the drop of batter sinks and slowly returns to the surface, the oil is not yet hot enough. If the batter drops to the bottom and immediately bounces up to the surface, the oil is ready for deep-frying. If the oil smokes, it has gotten too hot and the temperature should be lowered.

The oil used for deep-frying can be saved and used again. To grant your oil longer life, remove food crumbs with the fine mesh strainer during deep-frying. The quality of used oil is judged by its clarity, not by the number of times used nor the length of time used. Fresh oil is light yellow in color and clear. If the used oil is still relatively clear, it is salvageable and readily usable again. However, used oil which appears darker and clouded should be discarded because the temperature at which it will begin to smoke will drop and consequently, a high enough temperature cannot be achieved for proper deep-frying resulting in foods turning out very greasy.

To store the used oil, first strain with a fine mesh strainer. Then place the oil in a heatproof container if the oil is still hot. Allow the oil to cool, cover, and store in the refrigerator until ready to use again. Peanut oil or a good vegetable oil such as corn oil will have a longer usable life as well as possess qualities superior to other oils for purposes of deep-frying foods. None of the pure vegetable oils contain cholesterol and the use of a polyunsaturated oil is strongly recommended.

Follow the steps below for effective deep-frying:

1) Heat 3-4 cups of oil in the wok until a light haze forms at approximately 375 degrees.

2) Drop in foods and deep-fry until foods are cooked.

3) Adjust the temperature to maintain a constant frying temperature of 375 degrees. Begin by setting temperature on high; if the oil gets too hot (smokes), turn down temperature to medium high and back to high if the oil drops below 375 degrees.

4) Follow the instructions given in the recipe.

Roasting, Baking, or Broiling

These cooking methods are so common and ordinary as to require limited explanation.

Meats or rolls may be roasted or baked in the oven. When roasting meats, use a broiling pan or place a rack on the bottom of a pan to support the meat. Add a small amount of water to the bottom of the pan, making sure the meat is above the water level. The water will keep the meat moist and also keep the drippings from burning onto the broiling pan.

Follow the steps below for effective roasting, baking or broiling:

1) Preheat the oven to the required temperature.

2) Place all foods in the center of the oven to allow for even roasting.

3) Follow the instructions given in the recipe.

Steaming

Steaming is one of the most nutritious, not to mention convenient, methods of cooking foods, retaining more nutrients and natural flavor than other conventional means of cooking. Steamed foods seal in natural juices of meats and vegetables which are delicious served over rice.

There are many different types of steamers available. The wok with a cover will serve as a good steamer. Multi-tiered bamboo steamers may be purchased. However, a large pot with a cover will suffice for the purpose of steaming food.

Steaming racks are required to support and elevate the plate of bowl which contains food to be steamed in a wok. A round cake rack will serve just as well as commercially available steaming racks. You may even improvise, using a water chestnut can with both ends removed as a substitue for a steaming rack. The rack should be set in the center of the wok or pan.

Three to four cups of water should be sufficient for steaming with a wok and cover. The water level should be about one inch below the steaming rack. Cover the wok and bring the water to a full boil using the highest temperature setting on your stove (full steam). Place the plate or bowl containing the food atop the steaming rack. Make sure the boiling water does not flow over into the bowl or plate. If this does occur, reduce the water level under the steaming rack. After inserting the food, cover and bring water again to a full boil and turn the temperature down to medium high to maintain a constant flow or steam. Be sure there is enough room for the steam to circulate.

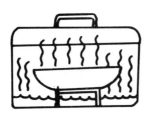

All steamers operate according to the same basic principle. The efficient circulation of steam is of paramount importance. Bamboo steamers have several tiers in which many dishes can be steamed simultaneously. The tiers and cover are set on top of a wok containing boiling water. There are also metal steamers consisting of a pot to hold the water and usually two tiers and a cover. For example, the bottom pot functions to cook soup stock while the two tiers are used to steam two other separate dishes. In this manner, many dishes may be steamed at one time saving both time and energy.

Follow the steps below for effective steaming.

1) Pour water in the wok or pot so that the water level stands one inch below the steaming rack or dish of food.

2) Cover the wok and bring the water to a full boil.

3) Use heatproof dishes only for steaming.

4) Insert the dish of food atop the steaming rack. Cover and bring to full boil (or full steam) again. Turn the temperature down to medium high and allow to steam for the specified time.

5) Check the water level when longer steaming times are necessary.

6) Follow the instructions given in the recipe.

MENU PLANNING

In serving a Chinese meal, there is no single main course as in the typical American meal, but a combination of courses to be presented simultaneously for everyone to enjoy. The Chinese serve two different types of meals depending upon the occasion and circumstances. The formal banquet dinner is appropriate for a larger group of people celebrating a special event while the more common informal dinner is more of a practical everyday meal. The recipes and emphasis of this book are directed toward the successful preparation of an informal Chinese meal and I would strongly suggest mastering the preparation of an informal dinner before attempting to serve a banquet.

A formal Chinese banquet is served to a gathering of ten or more guests customarily seated around a large round table with a revolving "Lazy Susan" in the center of the table for easy access to individual dinner courses by the guests. The banquet would normally consist of ten courses served in a particular order by a staff of servants. A large platter of cold meat and vegetable appetizers is usually first to arrive. Then follows two to four stir-fried dishes. The banquet always includes a hot soup which may be served at any point in the banquet, but traditionally near the end of the meal. The premier entrees such as a whole duck or fish would follow the stir-fried dishes. Rice or noodles would then be served to complete the banquet. All the dishes are brought out in quick succession to insure that all courses are hot and delicious. Finally, tea is served to end the banquet. Wine may also be served throughout the entire meal. The Chinese banquet is very elaborate and as such, should be reserved for very special occasions.

The informal Chinese dinner is more appropriately suited for the life styles of today. Nutritious, economical, and easy to prepare, Chinese food is most of all delicious. Therefore, I have devoted this book to the preparation of dishes used in an everyday Chinese meal. The informal dinner is designed for a party of four people. In any event, keep the group to less than ten people unless you plan to serve a buffet style dinner.

Planning your menu is the important first step in preparing the meal. Always prepare as much in advance as possible so as to be able to enjoy your company instead of being stuck in the kitchen. It is also a good practice to try a recipe before cooking it for guests. Always read the entire recipe before starting to cook.

MENU CHART

Number of People Served:	2	4	6	8	10
Course					
APPETIZER	*	*	*	*	*
SOUP	*	*	*	*	*
RICE or NOODLE	*	*	*	*	*
(Allow ½ cup uncooked or 1 ½ cups cooked rice per person)					
-BEEF	1	1	1	1	1
MEAT-CHICKEN			1	1	1
-PORK				1	1
(Selection of beef, chicken, or pork dish is up to you)					
SEAFOOD		1	1	1	1
VEGETABLE	1	1	1 ½	2	2 ½ or 3
DESSERT	*	*	*	*	*
(Usually fresh fruit)					

*ADJUST RECIPE FOR NUMBER OF PEOPLE.

The above menu chart illustrates sample menus for varying groups of people. For instance, an informal meal for four people would consist of one each of an appetizer, soup, rice or noodle, meat of your choice, seafood, and vegetable dish.

Generally, rice always accompanies a Chinese meal. Dessert is usually fresh fruit in season and tea is served at the end of the meal.

For every two additional people, i.e., 6, 8, 10, add one meat dish of your choice and increase the vegetable selection by ½ recipe. Rather than increase the recipe, you may prefer to make two different vegetable dishes. When in doubt as to how much food to prepare, remember it is far better to have leftovers than to run short of food at the dinner table.

When planning your menu, always consider the balance of flavors, the required ingredients, and cutting/cooking methods previously mentioned. Incorporate different meats and vegetables to vary the menu. For example, cook one dish of chicken, one dish of beef, and one dish of pork instead of three chicken dishes.

However, you may also economize by working the menu around one major roast or meat. By using a pork loin end roast for instance, portions of the roast can be cut for barbecued pork or sweet and sour pork. Bits and pieces of pork may further be used in the making of won ton filling or chow mein. The remaining bones may then be simmered for an excellent soup stock. Even the last bits of cooked pork on the bones can be removed and used in fried rice or egg fu yung. This efficient and economical use of meat also applies to the use of a whole chicken. Whenever possible, balance the menu by serving a different meat dish or use different meats in the vegetable dishes. You can always save what is not used for another meal with the aid of a freezer to preserve your meats.

The greatest assets in Chinese cooking are your resourcefulness, ingenuity, and ability to adapt in the face of unavailable ingredients. Shopping for weekly specials at your grocery store and preparing your menu accordingly will save you money. Of course, you may always choose to increase a recipe rather than prepare two separate recipes which will necessitate a shorter list of required ingredients.

CUSTOMS

An informal Chinese dinner is served with all the different courses placed at the center of the table simultaneously and everyone helps themselves.

An individual place setting is illustrated below.

1. Individual Plate — A luncheon or medium size plate to accommodate individual servings of food.
2. Individual Rice Bowl — A bowl used for soup initially and then used to hold rice. Two separate bowls may be used instead.
3. Small Plate — A dish used to hold soy sauce or dips.
4. Soup Spoon
5. Chopsticks — Bamboo, wood, or ivory utensils used for picking up food and eating.
6. Tea Cup — A small porcelain cup used for serving tea at the end of meal.
7. Wine Glass — A glass used for serving Chinese wine or any other wine throughout the meal.

Seating Arrangement

The seating arrangement is only important in serving a formal Chinese banquet. The guest of honor is seated at the head of the table which is situated furthest from the serving door while the host and/or hostess sits directly opposite facing the guest. People usually sit in any order they choose while participating in an informal Chinese dinner.

Order of service

The various courses of food should arrive at the table at nearly the same time and placed in the center of the table. Dishes are passed around and everyone serves themselves using either serving spoons or chopsticks. The particular order in which food courses are served in a formal Chinese banquet as earlier explained need not be adhered to in an informal Chinese dinner.

Beverages

The common beverages which accompany a Chinese meal are wine and tea. However, soup is also considered a beverage in a Chinese dinner. Soup is consumed throughout the meal. But for convenience in serving and minimizing dirty dishes, the Western custom of serving soup first may be followed. The same bowl may be used for soup, and then used for rice.

Wine

Wine served with a Chinese meal is a mere accompaniment to the diversity of flavors in Chinese foods. Shaohsing wine, a rice wine, served warm in porcelain cups, is the most popular wine. However, with so many good Western and European wines to select from, serve what appeals to the palates of you and your guests. Mr. R. Remlinger, a good friend and connoisseur of fine wines, suggests serving a chilled Rose as an all around complement to both Chinese meat and vegetable dishes.

Tea

Tea is the traditional drink served immediately before and after a Chinese meal. The choice of tea is entirely up to individiual tastes. There are basically three groups of teas.

Green tea — unfermented, dried in the sun. Delicate flavor and is light in color.

Oolong tea — partially fermented green tea imparting a slightly stronger flavor.

Red or Black tea — fermented teas which are first dried in the sun and then fired over charcoal. They possess the strongest flavor among the three varieties of tea.

The scented teas of which jasmine tea is by far the most popular, are made mostly from partially fermented tea.

Tea is properly brewed in porcelain pots and cups. Clean and heat the teapot by pouring in brisk boiling water and waiting until the teapot is warm before discarding the water. Next, add tea leaves and pour in fresh boiling water. Allow the covered tea to steep for approximately three minutes. The tea leaves may be reused for a second or even third brewing, but remember to leave some tea in the pot for the next brewing in order for the tea to release its full aroma.

Any tea will taste harsh and bitter if brewed too strong. The proportion of tea leaves to water will vary with the types of tea and the strength desired. Test a tea by varying the proportion of tea leaves to water until the desired taste is achieved. Do not brew the tea too strong, as Chinese tea drinkers do not add cream or sugar to their tea.

MENU SUGGESTIONS

The following sample menus were prepared with a group of six people in mind. Refer to the Menu chart in the Menu Planning section of this book for preparing meals for groups larger or smaller than six people.

I.   Egg Rolls
     Hot and Sour Soup
     Rice
     Ginger Beef
     Steamed Chicken with Mushrooms and Tiger Lily Buds
     Spicy Prawns
     Pork with Broccoli
     Tea

II. Barbecued Pork
     Tofu Soup
     Rice
     Black Bean Sauce Spareribs
     Stuffed Boneless Chicken Breast
     Jellyfish Cucumber Salad
     Beef with Asparagus
     Tea

III. Shrimp Stuffed Crab Claws
     Vegetable Soup
     Rice
     Barbecued Spareribs
     White Cut Chicken
     Poached Whole Fish
     Beef with Pea Pods
     Tea

IV. Spring Rolls
     Winter Melon Soup
     Rice
     Beef Tomato
     Roast Chicken
     Clams with Black Bean Sauce
     Chinese Greens with Shrimp
     Tea

V.   Foil Wrapped Chicken
     Spinach Soup
     Rice
     Oyster Sauce Beef
     Almond Breaded Chicken
     Shrimp Fu Yung
     Green Beans with Pork
     Tea

VI. Miniature Chicken Drumsticks
     Watercress Soup
     Rice
     Barbecued Pork
     Glazed Beef Steak·
     Sweet and Sour Fish
     Chicken Subgum
     Tea
VII. Shrimp Chips
     Egg Flower Soup
     Fried Rice
     Pork with Scrambled Eggs served with lettuce cups
     Sweet and Sour Chicken
     Foil Wrapped Fish
     Beef with Spinach
     Tea

For a buffet dinner, the following menus are recommended:

VIII. Barbecued Pork Buns
      Fried Rice
      Chicken Chow Mein
      Pineapple Beef Kabobs
      Sweet and Sour Spareribs
      Cucumber Salad with Shrimp
      Fruit Platter
      Tea

IX. Fried Won Tons with Sweet and Sour Sauce
     Siu Mai
     Shrimp Fried Rice
     Beef Chow Mein
     Soy Sauce Chicken
     Maifun Salad
     Pork Subgum
     Fresh Fruit Salad
     Tea

BASIC TIPS

These basic tips will save you time and make for the successful preparation of a Chinese Meal.

1. Thoroughly read the first chapter of this book, paying special attention to the **Cornstarch for Thickening** portion appearing in the Stir Frying section. Become acquainted with the techniques of cooking and the various equipment available to accomplish this purpose. Always read the entire recipe before you attempt to cook.

2. Organize in advance what you need to do. Decide which dishes can be kept warm and cook those courses first. Have all the required ingredients cut and measured for each dish and arranged on a tray such that everything will be on hand.

3. Slicing meat against the grain of the long muscle fibers will result in added tenderness when the meat is cooked. Partially frozen meat is easier to slice and more uniform slices can be obtained.

4. The use of garlic enhances the flavor of cooked food. With the wide blade of the cleaver, gently hit the clove of garlic, separating the skin which should be removed and discarded. Then crush the garlic with the blade of the cleaver. Crushed garlic may be added to most any dish. Just add the crushed garlic to oil heating in the wok. After the flavor has been released, the garlic may be removed or left in the wok while cooking the rest of the ingredients. Be careful not to burn the garlic.

5. Shaohsing wine and other rice wines may be replaced with dry sherry in most recipes. Recipes calling for mirin, a Japanese sweet rice wine, should not be replaced with Chinese rice wine. Chinese rice wine and mirin are not directly interchangeable.

6. Chicken stock may be used in place of water in recipes other than pastries, doughs, or sweet and sour dishes. This will result in a richer flavor. Canned chicken broth is a good substitute if you do not have time to make your own.

7. Dried forest mushrooms and other dried foods must be soaked in warm water before using in the recipe. They should be soaked until soft, removed, and then rinsed. The usual size of a medium mushroom after soaking is approximately three inches in diameter.

8. The recipes contained in this book were tested and developed using **Kikkoman** soy sauce which is considered a medium soy sauce. Use a medium soy sauce unless otherwise specified for best results.

9. A recipe requiring prawns will necessitate the proper shelling and deveining of the prawns. This is done by first removing the transparent shell. Cut open the top of the prawn to expose the black sandy vein. Remove the vein by gently pulling it out. The blue vein underneath the prawn should be left alone. Rinse the prawns and towel dry. Proceed with the recipe.

10. Always use your judgment in the substitution of ingredients called for in a recipe. Most ingredients used in this book are explained in the glossary. Be creative and do not be afraid to adapt the recipes to your own personal tastes.

"Dim Sum," literally translated, is dot of the heart, but more appropriately should be termed heart's delight.

A dim sum luncheon consists of bite-size meat and vegetable morsels which are steamed, pan fried, deep fried or baked, and served with tea. These small pieces of food can be enhanced by dipping in a selection of sauces, such as hot sauce, soy sauce, hot mustard, or vinegar dips.

Most restaurants usually serve dim sum between the hours of 11:00 A.M. to 3:00 P.M. Carts filled with the appetizers are constantly circulated throughout the restaurant. Stop the waitress and make your selections. After the meal, the small plates are counted and totalled. Eat slowly and enjoy!

All dishes included in this section are part of "Dim Sum." Serve some of the dishes as appetizers before a meal or as a part of the main portion of a Chinese meal. Naturally, the sweet items can be served as desserts.

Fresh fruits in season also make very nice desserts. A visit to a Chinese bakery if there is one in your area will provide a maximum selection of Chinese dessert items.

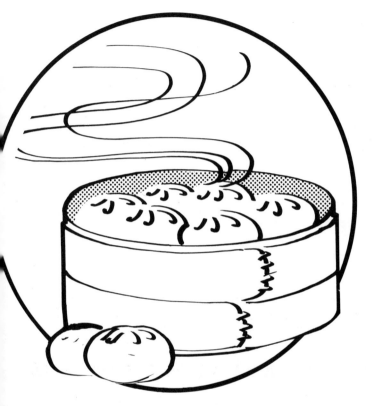

Dim Sum & Appetizers

SWEET AND SOUR SAUCE
(1½ C Sauce)

¾ C   water
1½ T   cornstarch
2 T   rice vinegar
3 T   catsup
⅔ C   sugar
dash of soy sauce

1. Mix together all ingredients in order.
2. Cook and stir until sauce comes to a full boil.
3. Pour into bowl to use with appetizers.

•

Mix sauce together ahead. Bring to full boil just before serving. Sauce can be kept warm or reheated.

PRAWN CRACKERS OR SHRIMP CHIPS

     shrimp chips
2"   peanut oil 375° F

1. Drop chips into hot oil and cook about 5 seconds or until puffed.
2. Remove and drain on paper towels.
3. Allow to cool and store like potato chips.

•

Shrimp chips may be purchased in most oriental food stores or super markets. Will keep about a week in air-tight containers. Fry ahead and keep airtight in freezer. No reheating required.

Uncooked chips keep up to one year in a dry place. Use chips as a garnish for any meat dish such as roast chicken, or spareribs.

SPRING ROLLS
(25 rolls)

25   Won Ton Wrappers

Filling

1 T   oil
½ C   chopped Chinese sausage or ham
½ C   chopped onions
¼ C   chopped celery
½ C   chopped fresh mushrooms
¼ C   chopped bamboo shoots
1 C   beansprouts
1 T   Soy Sauce
1 T   mirin
¼ t   salt

1   egg white (to seal wrappers)
2"   oil for deep frying 375°

1. Heat oil in wok. Cook Chinese sausage for ½ min. Add remaining filling ingredients and toss. Cook on high heat for 1 minute.

2. Remove from wok, drain off excess liquid. Allow filling to cool.

3. Put 1 tablespoon filling ingredients on wrapper and fold, sealing with egg white.

4. Fry in 375° oil until golden brown (2-3 min.)

5. Serve with sweet and sour sauce. (pg. 34)

To fold:

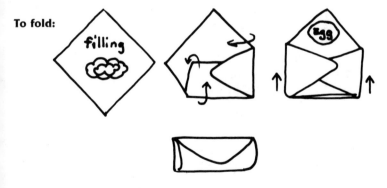

May be made ahead, reheat in 375° oven 5 minutes.

FRIED WON TON
(20 Won Tons)

20   won ton wrappers
2"   peanut oil — 375°

1. Fold won tons
2. Deep fry until golden brown
3. Drain
4. Serve with sweet and sour sauce. (pg. 34)

A.   Cut 1" slit

B.   Take top two corners and pull through the slit forming a bow tie

•

1 lb. won ton wrappers contain approximately 50 wrappers. Freeze unused wrappers. Fry ahead and reheat in oven. Good cold with sweet and sour sauce.

Dust won tons with powdered sugar. Put sugar in paper bag. As soon as won tons are fried, put in bag and shake to coat with sugar.

FRIED WON TON
(Stuffed)
(50 won tons)

1 lb   package of Won Ton wrappers

Filling

½ lb   ground pork
¼ C   chopped onions
1   Chinese sausage chopped
½C   chopped bamboo shoots
½ C   chopped green onions
1 t   mirin or rice wine
1 t   salt
1 t   soy sauce
2 t   cornstarch

1   egg white
2"   oil for deep frying (375°)
         Sweet and Sour sauce (pg. 34)

1. Combine filling ingredients.
2. Place 1 t filling in wrapper and fold according to instructions, sealing with egg white.
3. Fry in oil for 2 minutes until golden brown, turning occasionally. Serve with Sweet and Sour Sauce.

To fold: A. Place 1 t filling on center of wrapper and fold in half, sealing edges with egg white.
          B. Put small dab of egg white on one corner and bring both corners together, press corners to seal.

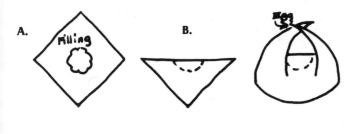

May stop after step A. and fry as triangles

Fry ahead and reheat in oven (375° 5 min.)

EGG ROLLS
(10-12 rolls)

Egg roll skins (10-12 skins)

2 T	cornstarch dissolved in ¼ C water
4	eggs
½ t	salt
	oil

1. Combine cornstarch mixture, eggs and salt. Beat until well blended.

2. Pour a small amount of oil into an 8" teflon or non-sticky frying pan. Rub oil in with a paper towel. Reserve paper towel.

3. Heat skillet on medium heat until hot.

4. Pour small amount of egg mixture into skillet and coat bottom of pan with egg mixture. Quickly pour excess out, back into bow.

    Cook until edge pulls from sides of pan. Remove from the pan and set aside. Continue until all of egg mixture is used, oiling the skillet as needed.

●

Skins may be made ahead. Stack together, roll into a cylinder, wrap air tight and freeze. Defrost and use when needed. These skins will not brown without dipping egg rolls into batter before deep frying.

If store bought wrappers must be used, try to use the thinnest wrappers available. Store bought egg roll wrappers need not be dipped into batter before deep frying.

Egg roll filling

2 T	oil
1 C	lean pork sliced thin
½ C	chopped onions
1 C	beansprouts
½ C	chopped celery
¼ C	chopped bamboo shoots
2 T	chopped water chestnuts
2 lg.	forest mushrooms, sliced (soaked until soft and rinsed)
½ t	salt or to taste
1 T	oyster sauce
½ C	water or soup stock
	cornstarch for thickening

To Cook Filling:

1. Heat oil in wok until hot. Add pork and cook until all pink is gone (2 min.)

2. Add all other ingredients except cornstarch, cover, bring to boil and cook 1 minute.

3. Thicken with cornstarch and water to form a fairly thick sauce. Set aside and allow to cool. Refrigerate until ready to use.

Batter

½ C   flour
¼ C   cornstarch
1 t   baking powder
½ t   baking soda
¾ C   cold water

2"   oil for deep frying (375°)

1. **To wrap egg rolls:** Place about 3 T of filling on the lower bottom of round wrapper. If using square wrappers, place like a diamond in front of you. Bring bottom up to cover filling and roll once. Fold sides in to overlap. Place a small amount of batter at top of wrapper to seal. Continue to roll wrapper until closed. (If no batter is available, mix small amount of flour with water to use as seal.)

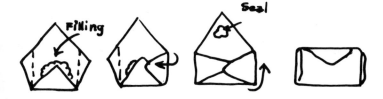

2. Mix together to batter.

3. Heat 2" of oil in wok to 375°.

4. Dip each egg roll into batter and deep fry in oil for 2 minutes or until golden brown. Turn egg rolls as soon as possible to keep top from breaking open. Continue turning to fry evenly.

5. Remove and serve as soon as possible.

6. Remove bits of batter from oil with a mesh strainer and continue to fry remaining egg rolls in the same manner. If oil gets too hot, turn to medium high. Always try to maintain 375°.

●

Wrappers may be prepared ahead and frozen, or complete through step 4 and freeze. Defrost before dipping in batter to deep fry. Egg rolls can also be battered and partially fried, remove, allow to cool and refrigerate. Finish browning egg rolls when ready to serve. Oil must not be too hot or outside will be too brown and the inside will be cold. If oil is smoking, it is too hot.

Egg rolls **do not** reheat well in the oven. Best served as soon as they are done.

GAI LUNG
(Deep fried pork turnovers)
(24 turnovers)

Filling:

2 T	oil
½ C	finely diced pork or ground pork
¼ C	dried shrimp (soaked ½ hr. in hot water, drained, and chopped)
1 lg.	forest mushroom (soaked, rinsed, and chopped)
1 T	red bean curd (optional)
½ t	salt or to taste
1	chopped green onion

To prepare filling:

1. Heat oil in wok and cook pork until done. (About 2 minutes). Add shrimp, onions, celery, mushrooms and cook 1 minute.

2. Add red bean curd and salt. Cook until all ingredients are well blended. Stir in green onions, remove and allow to cool before wrapping.

Dough:

2 C	glutinous rice flour
¼ C	mashed potato flakes
½ t	salt
1 C	boiling water
¼ C	all purpose flour (for dusting)
¼ C	sesame seeds
2"	oil for deep frying (375°)

To prepare dough:

1. Combine rice flour, mashed potato flakes, and salt in a bowl. Add boilng water, mix well and knead until smooth, adding extra **rice flour** if needed.

To assemble

1. Divide dought into 24 walnut-size balls, roll in palm of hands until round.

2. Press on sesame seeds on outside only, and dust with **all purpose flour**. Flatten to form 3" circle, ¼ inch thick.

3. Fill with 1 T filling. Fold in half and close edges by pinching dough together. May also crimp edge like pie crust. Dust with more all purpose flour if needed. Set on a tray and cover w/ foil. Keep refrigerated until ready to deep fry.

4. Deep fry in 2 inches of oil, 325°, for approximately 6-8 minutes, turning constantly.

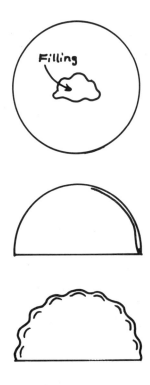

Substitue equal amounts of chopped Chinese sausage or ham for the dried shrimp.

STEAMED MEATBALLS
(18-20 meatballs)

1 lb   ground pork
¼ C   chopped green onions
1 t   salt
1   egg white
2 T   cornstarch
1 t   sesame seed oil
1 t   rice wine

1. Chop all ingredients until a paste is formed. (Best done in food processor.)
2. Shape into 1½" meatballs with a wet spoon. Place on a steaming plate.
3. Steam for 15 minutes. Serve hot. Use soy sauce and hot mustard as a dip.

●

Different meats and vegetables may be used instead of pork and green onions.

STEAMED MEATBALLS WITH
SWEET RICE
(18-20 meatballs: 4 servings)

¾ C	sweet rice (washed and soaked in water for at least 3 hours) Drained.
¾ lb	lean ground pork
2 T	chopped water chestnuts
2	med forest mushrooms chopped (soaked & rinsed)
1 ½ t	salt
1 t	mirin or rice wine
1 T	cornstarch
	soy sauce for dipping

1. Combine pork with water chestnuts, mushrooms, salt, mirin, and cornstarch. Shape into 1 inch meatballs. Wet hands for easier handling.

2. Roll meatballs to cover with sweet rice.

3. Set meatballs one inch apart on a steaming plate.

4. Place in a steamer, cover, bring water to a full boil, reduce temperature to medium high and steam for 20 minutes.

5. Serve with soy sauce as dip.

•

Substitute other meats. Recipe may be prepared ahead and reheated by the same method of steaming just until hot.

HA GOW
(Shrimp Dumpling)

Filling

¾ lb   shrimp shelled, deveined and chopped
¼ C   bamboo shoots chopped
1 t   salt
1 t   sesame seed oil
½ t   sugar
1   egg white
2 T   cornstarch

Combine filling ingredients and set in refrigerator for one hour.

Dough

1 C   wheat starch
½ C   tapioca starch
½ t   salt

1 C   boiling water
2 T   oil

1. Mix wheat starch, tapioca starch and salt together in a large pot.

2. Make a well in center and pour in boiling water. Stir to moisten ingredients, cover pot and allow to rest 10 min.

3. Knead until a smooth dough forms adding oil. Set aside. Keep covered until ready to use.

4. Roll portions of dough into a long roll and cut walnut size pieces. Roll each piece in hand until smooth.

5. Generously oil cleaver and counter top. Press out dough to form a 3-inch circle. (Or use a tortilla press.)

6. Pleat half of circle to form a pouch. Put in 2 teaspoons of filling, cover and pinch ends together.

7. Gently curve dumpling to form a crescent.

8. Place on an oiled steaming plate and steam 15 min.

Dough can be made ahead. Wrap with foil or plastic wrap. Dough keeps one day at room temperature.

Dumplings may be made 1 day ahead. Cover tightly and refrigerate. Keeps longer after steaming. Reheat by resteaming. Suzanne Chan's favorite.

SIU MAI
(30 Siu Mai)

30   Siu Mai wrappers

Filling ingredients:

1 lb	coarse ground pork
1	Chinese sausage chopped
2 T	bamboo shoots chopped
2 T	water chestnuts chopped
¼ C	onions chopped
2 lg	forest mushrooms chopped (soaked and rinsed)
1½ t	salt
½ t	sugar
1 t	wine
1 t	sesame seed oil
1 t	soy sauce
2 T	cornstarch

1. Combine all filling ingredients.
2. Place 1 T filling in center of wrapper.
3. Gather edge of wrapper around filling. Flatten the bottom, squeeze the center and smooth off the top with wet fingers.
4. Place on steaming plate ½" apart.
5. Steam for 20 min.

•

May be prepared through step 4 and refrigerate. Also delicious reheated.

POT STICKERS
(40-50)

½ pkg. Siu Mai wrappers (8 oz. pkg. contains about 80 wrappers).

Filling

1 lb	ground pork
2 C	chopped nappa
¼ C	chopped onions
1 T	chopped ginger root
1 t	soy sauce
1 t	salt
2 t	sesame seed oil
1 t	wine
½ t	sugar
2 T	cornstarch
	oil for frying
3 C	chicken soup stock

1. Combine filling ingredients.
2. Place 2 t filling in center of wrapper, wet edge and seal to form a half circle.
3. Hold top edge and press down to flatten bottom.
4. Heat a 12" skillet with small amount of oil and fry pot stickers on medium high heat until brown on all sides.
5. Pour in ½ C soup stock, cover and cook until liquid is absorbed.
6. Repeat process to cook the rest of the pot stickers.
7. Serve with soy sauce or vinegar dip, or hot sesame seed oil.

•

To make vinegar dip, just add a few drops of rice vinegar to soy sauce. 8 oz. pkg. contains 80 wrappers. Freeze remainder of pkg.

Filling may be prepared ahead and refrigerated. Fill pot stockers, brown them and then they can be frozen. To reheat, allow to defrost, refry for one minute and continue with the recipe.

BARBECUED PORK FILLING
(Fills 32 buns)

1 T	oil
½ C	diced onions
1 lg	forest mushroom (soaked, rinsed and diced)
2 T	hoisin sauce
2 T	catsup
1½ T	sugar
1 T	oyster sauce
¼ t	garlic powder
½ t	salt
½ C	water

1 T   cornstarch dissolved in 1 T water

1½ C diced cooked barbecued pork

1. Add oil to wok, cook onions and mushrooms on high heat for ½ minute.
2. Add all other ingredients, except cornstarch and barbecued pork, Allow to cook ½ minute.
3. Thicken with cornstarch mixture to form a thick sauce. Mix in diced pork.
4. Allow mixture to cool before filling buns.

●

Filling may be made ahead. Freeze unused portion.

CHA SIEW BAO
(Steam Barbecued Pork Buns)
(Or Hum Bao)
(16 buns)

½ C	warm water
1 T	sugar
2 T	dry yeast
¾ C	warm milk
½ C	sugar
3-3½	C all purpose flour
½ t	salt
1 t	baking powder
1 T	shortening

16 sq of waxed paper (3" x 3")

½   recipe of barbecued pork filling (pg. 47)

1. In a large bowl, dissolve sugar and yeast in warm water. Allow mixture to sit 5 minutes.

2. Combine warm milk with ½ cup sugar, stir to dissolve sugar. Add to yeast mixture.

3. Combine 3 cups of flour with the salt. Stir into liquid yeast mixture.

4. Stir until a firm dough is formed. Turn out on floured surface and knead until smooth, adding extra flour if necessary. (About 10 minutes).

5. Sprinkle baking powder over dough and knead in. Knead in 1 Tablespoon shortening, adding extra flour to keep from sticking. Place in a greased bowl, turn dough over and cover with a towel Allow to rise until doubled in bulk.

6. Punch down dough, knead 2 minutes and allow dough to rest 2 minutes. Cut into 16 equal pieces.

7. Roll each piece into a ball, then roll into a 4 inch circle, dusting with flour if necessary. Allow dough to rest 2 minutes. Roll out other pieces while waiting.

8. Place 1 heaping tablespoon of filling in center of dough. Pull dough over filling and close top by pleating, pinching and twisting edges together.

9. Place on a piece of waxed paper, pleated edge down. Space 2 inches apart on a steaming plate. Allow to rise 45 minutes in a warm oven (95°).

10. Steam in wok for 15 minutes at full steam.

11. Remove cover carefully so water will not drop on top of buns.

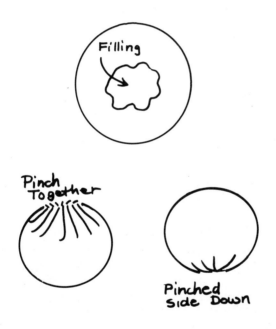

Be careful not to pull dough too much or tops of buns will be too thin.

Complete entire recipe ahead. Buns can be frozen and reheated by steaming until hot. Use other filling ingredients such as cooked Chinese sausage or sweet bean paste.

BAKED BARBECUED PORK BUNS
(Baked Hum Bao)
(16 Buns)

2 T   dry yeast
¼ C   warm water (110°)
1 T   sugar

½ C   warm milk
¼ C   melted butter or margarine
½ C   sugar
1 t   salt
2 lg   eggs (room temp.)

3-3½ C all purpose flour (or use high protein flour)

1   egg white beaten with 2 t water

2 T   melted butter

16   pieces waxed paper (3" x 3")

½   recipe of barbecued pork filling (pg. 47)

1. In a large bowl, dissolve yeast in warm water and stir in 1 T sugar. Allow mixture to sit 10 minutes.
2. Combine warm milk, melted butter, sugar, salt and eggs. Add to yeast mixture and beat together.
3. Add 2 cups of the flour to make a thick batter, beat until smooth.
4. Gradually mix in enough of the remaining flour (about 1 C) to make a stiff dough. Turn out onto a floured surface; knead until smooth (about 10 minutes), working in remaining ½ C of flour as needed to keep dough from sticking.
5. Place dough in a greased bowl, turn dough over, cover and allow to rise in a warm place until doubled in bulk.

6. Punch down dough, knead 2 minutes and allow dough to rest 2 minutes. Cut into 16 equal pieces.

7. Roll each piece into a ball, then roll into a 4 inch circle, dusting with flour if necessary. Allow dough to rest 2 minutes. Roll out other pieces while waiting.

8. Place 1 heaping tablespoon of filling in center of dough. Pull dough over filling and close top by pleating, pinching and twisting edge together.

9. Place on piece of waxed paper, pleated edge down. Space 2 inches apart on a cookie sheet. Allow to rise 45 minutes in a warm oven (95°).

10. Brush gently with egg white mixture. Bake at 350° for 15 minutes or until golden brown.

11. Remove from oven and brush immediately with melted butter. For a sweeter taste, brush with honey too.

●

Use a high protein flour specially for baking bread for best results instead of all purpose flour.

Baked hum bows may be made ahead through step 11. Freeze or keep refrigerated until needed. To serve, reheat in a 325° oven for about 10 minutes and brush again with melted butter. Allow frozen hum bows to defrost before reheating.

BAKED BARBECUED PORK BUNS
(Quick Method)
(20-24 Buns)

2 loaves of frozen unbaked bread, defrosted

20-24 squares of waxed paper (3" x 3")

Filling

1 T	oil
½ C	diced pork or ground pork
½ C	chopped onions
2 lg	forest mushrooms (soaked, rinsed and chopped)
2 T	hoisin sauce
2 T	catsup
1½ T	sugar
1 t	soy sauce
½ t	garlic powder
½ t	salt
½ C	water

cornstarch and water for thickening

1   egg white beaten with 2 t water

¼ C   melted butter

To prepare filling

1. Heat oil in the wok until hot. Add the pork and cook until done (2-3 min.).
2. Add all other ingredients except cornstarch, bring to a boil and thicken with cornstarch and water to form a thick sauce.

To make buns

1. Cut each loaf of dough into 10-12 equal pieces. Roll each piece into a ball, then roll into a 4 inch circle. Allow dough to rest 5 minutes. Roll out other pieces while waiting.

2. Hold one piece of dough in palm of hand and place 1 heaping tablespoon of filing in the center of the piece of dough.

3. Pull dough over filling and close top by pleating, pinching and twisting edge together.

4. Place the filled bun on a piece of waxed paper, pleated side down. Repeat until all dough is used.

5. Space 2 inches apart on a cookie sheet and allow to rise 45 minutes in a warm oven (95°).

6. Brush tops of buns with egg white mixture. Bake at 375° for 15-20 minutes, or until golden brown.

7. Remove from oven and immediately brush with melted butter.

●

Other meats and vegetables may be used. Make buns ahead and keep in freezer. Defrost, cover with foil and reheat in a 300° degree oven for about 15 minutes. Brush with melted butter again.

CHINESE SAUSAGE BAO
(16 buns)

8 Chinese sausages

1   recipe of steamed or baked bread dough

1   egg white beaten with 2 t water (to brush tops of buns for baking)
¼ C   melted butter (to brush buns after baking)

16   pieces of waxed paper (3" x 3")

1. Steam Chinese sausages for 15 minutes. Remove and cut each sausage in half.
2. Prepare one recipe of steamed or baked bread dough. Allow to rise according to instructions. Divide dough into 16 equal pieces.
3. Roll each piece into a 3 inch circle. Place one piece of sausage in the center, fold sides in to overlap, leaving ends open.
4. Place on a piece of waxed paper, folded sides down.
5. Allow to rise in a warm oven (95°) for 45 minutes.

To Bake:

Brush tops with beaten egg white mixture. Bake at 350° for 15 minutes. Remove and brush with melted butter.

To Steam:

Steam in wok for 15 minutes. Do not use beaten egg white or melted butter to brush tops of buns.

•

Buns may be made ahead and reheated.

CHICKEN ROLLS
(24 rolls)

Filling

2 T	oil
1 C	chicken breast
2 lg	black forest mushrooms
½ C	bamboo shoots
½ C	onions
2 T	oyster sauce
¼ t	salt
8	sheets phyllo
¼ C	oil

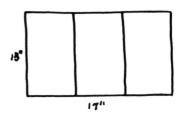

1. Soak mushrooms to soften and rinse.

2. Slice chicken, mushrooms, bamboo shoots, and onions into thin strips.

3. Heat oil in wok and cook chicken until meat turns white. Add mushrooms, bamboo shoots, and onions, cook ½ min. Add oyster sauce and salt. Mix thoroughly and remove. Allow mixture to cool before wrapping.

4. Cut each phyllo sheet into thirds. Take one piece and brush half of sheet with oil, fold in half to form a square. Brush with more oil.

5. Place 1 T filling in lower corner. Fold corner up to cover filling, then roll up once, fold both sides in to overlap, continue rolling up, Brush entire surface with oil.

6. Place on cookie sheet and bake at 400° for 15 minutes or until golden brown.

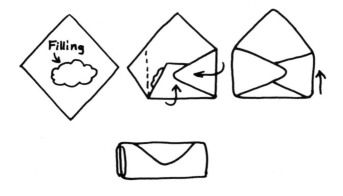

CURRY TURNOVERS
(24 turnovers)

Filling

1 T	oil
½ lb	ground beef or pork
½ C	chopped onions
½ C	chopped bamboo shoots
1-2 t	curry
¾ t	salt
¼ t	sugar
1 T	catsup

8	sheets of phyllo pastry 13" x 17"

½ C	oil

1. Heat 1 T oil in wok, brown meat, drain off excess fat.
2. Add all other ingredients and mix together; cook 2 minutes. Remove and allow to cool.
3. Cut phyllo sheets into thirds lengthwise and stack. Keep moist by covering with waxed paper and damp towel.

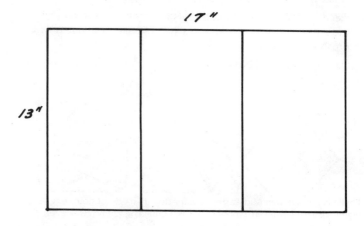

4. Take one strip, brush half of strip with oil and fold in half lengthwise. Brush top surface with oil and place one heaping teaspoon of filling on bottom of strip.

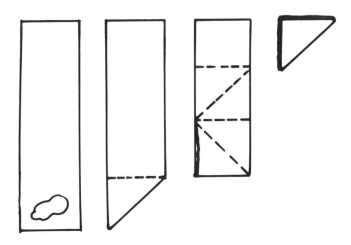

5. Fold strip over filling so bottom of strip meets left side. Continue folding at right angles. Tuck at top to form triangle.

6. Brush top and bottom of triangle with oil.

7. Repeat until all dough and filling is used. Place on cookie sheet and bake at 400° for 15 minutes or until golden brown. Also may be fried in oil until golden brown.

●

May be made ahead and freeze. Keeps well cooked. Defrost before reheating in oven.

Reheat at 375° for 5 or 10 minutes.

Phyllo is a tissue thin Mid-Eastern pastry dough, made of flour, egg and water. Usually comes in 1 pound boxes, containing about 20 sheets rolled up. Check edges to be sure of freshness, should be smooth, not crumbly. To keep from drying during wrapping, spread damp towel on counter. Place a sheet of waxed paper over towel, put phyllo sheets on top, cover with another sheet of waxed paper and damp towel. Make sure phyllo sheets are not directly touching damp towel.

SESAME SEED PUFFS
(Tay Doy)
(25 puffs)

3¼ C   sweet rice flour or 1 lb.

⅓ C   mashed potato flakes

1 C   brown sugar

1 C   boiling water

1 C   sweet red bean paste (chilled and made into ¾ inch balls)

¼ C   sesame seeds

2"   oil for deep frying (350°, medium high)

1. Pour 3 C sweet rice flour into a large bowl, reserving the ¼ cup for later use.

2. Mix potato flakes with flour mixture in bowl. Add brown sugar and stir to mix ingredients.

3. Add 1 C hot water and stir all ingredients together until cool enough to handle. Knead until dough is smooth, dusting with extra rice flour.

4. Divide dough in half, roll out into sausage 1½" in diameter and cut into 12 equal pieces. Roll each piece in palms until round. Press ball into sesame seeds, one side only, and gently flatten. Sesame seeds should be on outside of puff.

5. Use the ¼ C reserved flour to dust hands and dough to keep from sticking. Shape into cup large enough to fill with one ball of sweet red bean paste. Close off top to reform a ball. Set aside until ready to deep fry.

6. Repeat with other pieces of dough.

7. Place six puffs in 350° oil, allow to fry 1 min. gently turning puffs constantly with a slotted spoon. After one minute, begin to press each puff against the side of wok and then turn over. Continue frying in this manner until golden brown. (Approx. 5 min.) Remove and drain on paper towel.

•

Oil must not be too hot. Leftover dough may be frozen for later use.

Sweet red bean paste is usually found canned. 1 can contains 18 ounces or about 2 cups.

Julianne Chan's favorite.

STEAMED SPONGE CAKE
(1 9" cake)

4 lg	eggs (at room temperature)
1 C	sugar
1 C	sifted cake flour
¼ t	baking powder
1 t	vanilla
1 t	sesame seeds
1 pc	of waxed paper to fit bottom of 9 inch round cake pan

1. Separate eggs and beat egg whites until stiff. (Set aside.)

2. Combine sugar and egg yolks. Beat until well blended (5 minutes at medium speed).

3. Add flour, baking powder and vanilla, beat 3 minutes at low speed. Add egg whites and beat 5 minutes at medium speed. Turn to high speed and beat ½ minute.

4. Pour into a 9" ungreased cake pan lined with waxed paper. Sprinkle with sesame seeds.

5. Place pan on a rack in a wok with boiling water, cover and steam on medium high heat for 20 minutes. Remove.

6. Allow cake to cool 2 minutes, turn out and peel off waxed paper from bottom of cake. Serve warm or cold.

●

Cake may be made ahead and kept airtight for up to 2 days.

EGG CUSTARD TARTS
(24 tarts)

Pastry

1¾ C	all purpose flour, sifted
½ C	butter (1 cube)
1 T	sugar
1	egg
1 t	vanilla

Custard

⅔ C	sugar
1½ C	hot water
5	eggs
1 t	vanilla
1 t	rice vinegar

To make pastry

1. Knead butter and sugar together on a pastry board, adding egg and vanilla.

2. Gently work in flour and knead into a smooth dough. Do not over knead.

3. On a floured board, roll dough into a ¼" inch thick sheet and cut into rounds to fit tart pans.

4. Place dough into tart pans with the flour side up to hold custard. Gently fit into tart pan and flute edge, cutting off excess dough.

To make filling

1. Dissolve sugar in hot water and allow to cool.

2. Beat eggs, vanilla and vinegar together and gradually add to the cooled sugar mixture. Stir well to combine.

3. Strain mixture and set aside.

To make tarts

1. Place tart pans on a cookie sheet and carefully pour custard filling into tart pans.

2. Bake at 425° for 20 minutes.

Serve hot or cold.

FORTUNE COOKIES
(12-15 cookies)

1 C	cake flour
3 T	sweet rice flour or cornstarch
½ C	sugar
dash	salt
½ C	salad oil
3	egg whites
1 t	vanilla
¼ C	water

Fortunes on paper

1. Combine cake flour, rice flour, sugar and salt in a mixing bowl.

2. Add oil and egg whites, blend until smooth, add vanilla and gradually stir in water.

3. Drop rounded teaspoons of batter onto a lightly oiled cookie sheet. Spread batter with spoon to a 3" round. (Make only six at a time.)

4. Bake 15 minutes at 300° until light brown.

5. Place fortune on cookie, fold in half and quickly bend. If cookies harden before folding, quickly place in oven to reheat. Then bending is easier.

HINT: Wear gloves!

●

Use the edge of a coffee can to bend cookies and then place in a muffin pan to keep cookie from unfolding. Cookies may be made larger, too.

The role of soup in a Chinese meal is that of a beverage served throughout the meal, but traditionally towards the end of the meal.

Soups

BASIC CHICKEN STOCK I
(from bones)
(yield: 6 C)

1	carcass of chicken or 3 cups bones
8C	water
2	slices ginger root
1	scallion

1. Place the bones, ginger, scallion, and the water in a pot and bring to a full boil on high heat.

2. Skim froth and fat, turn temperature to simmer, cover and simmer stock for 1 hour.

3, Remove bones and strain soup stock with a fine mesh strainer. Cheesecloth may be used if desired.

4. Skim soup of excess fat. Allow soup to cool, then refrigerate. Fat will harden on the surface and can be easily removed with a strainer.

•

Salt is usually not added until soup stock is used. Soup stock can be used in place of water in most recipes, making the dish more flavorful. Canned chicken broth is a good substitute.

Stock may be stored in the refrigerator for up to 5 days. Freeze stock in ice cube trays, then store in plastic bags and use as needed.

Use pork bones to make pork soup stock or a combination of pork and chicken bones. Increase water and simmering time for larger bones.

The proper proportion of water to bones is just enough water to cover the bones, if enough bones have been accumulated.

Use beef stock only for beef dishes.

A whole chicken can be used instead of bones. After cooking, reserve chicken for another use.

BASIC SOUP STOCK II
(from meat)
(Yield: 4 cups)

4 C   water
1 C   meat, sliced thin or minced. (Usually pork loin, or chicken)
1 t   salt or to taste.

1. Bring water to a full boil and add meat. Stir to break apart.
2. Skim any froth on surface, and cook until meat is done. (5 min.)
3. Add salt to taste or any other seasonings desired.

●

This is a very fast and easy way to make soup stock. Increase ingredients to obtain desired amount of soup. Also a very good way to use meat as part of the soup. Just vary vegetables used to produce a different soup.

Example: Add nappa or celery cabbage and cook for extra minute. Now you have pork or chicken nappa soup.

Most family style soups are made this way.

SOUP VARIATIONS

Soups made with basic soup stocks using either method. 4 C of soup stock seasoned with salt: (4-6 servings)

1. **Winter melon soup**

    ½ lb. winter melon. Remove hard outer skin and seeds. Dice in ½ inch cubes. Add some diced black forest mushrooms for color and flavor. (Soak and rinse mushrooms first). Bring soup stock to a full boil, add all ingredients, cover and cook slowly for 10 minutes.

2. **Hairy melon soup**

    1 medium melon (about 1 ½ cups sliced). Peel and rinse melon. Slice into ¼ inch thick slices and cook soup 10 min. (1" x 1" x ¼") slices.

3. **Bean cake or tofu soup**

½ lb. or 1 C tofu cut into small squares. Try to add some amount of green vegetable to help the color. Cook gently for 1 min.

4. **Nappa, bok choy, peapod, watercress, spinach.**

Bring soup stock to a boil and add the desired vegetable, sliced in small pieces, and cook until done (1 or 2 minutes). Vegetables cook very fast. Try to retain green color.

●

All of the above soups are prepared basically the same way. Vary the ingredients to vary the soup. Use different garnishes such as cooked ham or crab to make soups more elegant. Soups are usually served with the dinner, but to make serving easier, serve soup before the main dishes.

WON TON SOUP
(2 servings as complete meal;
6-8 servings as dinner soup)

25 Won Ton wrappers

Filling

½ C	ground pork (unseasoned)
½ C	prawns, shelled and deveined
2 T	water chestnuts
2 T	bamboo shootys
½ t	salt
1 t	cornstarch
1 t	rice wine
1	egg white to seal wrappers

Soup

8-10 C chicken stock (seasoned with 1 t salt or to taste)
2 med forest mushrooms, (soaked until soft, rinsed and sliced)

½ C	sliced bamboo shots
¼ C	sliced water chestnuts
2 C	sliced Chinese greens (bok choy) or any green leafy veg.
¼ C	chopped green onions

1. **To prepare filling:** Chop ground pork, prawns, water chestnuts and bamboo shoots until smooth. Add salt, cornstarch and wine mix until smooth, refrigerate until ready to wrap won tons.
2. Wrap won tons according to instructions.
3. Boil won tons in a large pot of boilng water for 2 minutes, remove and rinse in cold water, drain. Set aside.
4. Bring chicken stock to a boil, adding salt, bamboo shoots, water chestnuts and mushrooms.
5. Add won tons to soup, bring to a boil, reduce temperature and cook 5 minutes.
6. Add green vegetables during last minute of cooking. Toss green onions on top to garnish.

To wrap won tons

A. Place 1 heaping teaspoon of filling on the top corner of wrapper.

B. Fold tip of wrapper over the meat. Roll wrapper until halfway down covering meat.

C. Put a small dab of egg on the left hand side of covered meatball.

D. Pull sides back and pinch together, placing one side on top of the egg white.

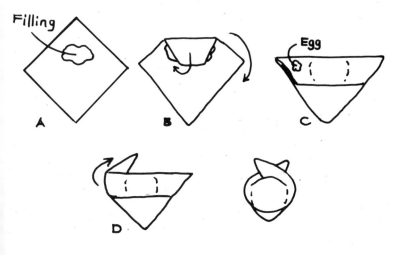

Prepare filling ahead and freeze, or freeze after wrapping through step 2. To freeze: Wrap won tons, place on a tray in a single layer, making sure they are not touching. When frozen, remove from tray and place in an air tight freezer container. May keep frozen up to one month. Cook them later straight from a frozen state as though they were just wrapped.

To cut steps down even more, won tons may be prepared through step 3. Then they can either be frozen in small packages of 8 or 10. To use, must allow to defrost and then continue with the recipe. Or prepare through step 3 and keep covered with water in the refrigerator. Use as soon as possible. Remember, this is recommended only if you are entertaining and time is limited.

Handling of won ton wrappers

Won ton wrappers are sold fresh or frozen, thick or thin, usually in one pound packages. If frozen, defrost, take out the amount needed and wrap the remainder air tight and may refreeze only one time. Fresh wrappers keep one week in the refrigerator. Always cover wrappers from the air to keep from drying out. The white powder on the wrappers is cornstarch. Always keep the side with more cornstarch on the outside when wrapping, so it will cook out.

SEAWEED SOUP
(4-6 servings)

4 C	water or soup stock
½ C	ground pork
½ C	chopped prawns (shelled, deveined and cleaned)
1 t	salt
4	water chestnuts chopped
3	sheets of dried seaweed (tear into small pieces)
1	egg beaten
1	green onion chopped
1 t	sesame seed oil

1. Bring water to boil.
2. Add about ½ C of boilng water to the ground pork and prawns to break up meat. Add to the boiling water in the pot and stir to break up meat.
3. Add salt, water chestnuts, simmer 5 minutes.
4. Add seaweed and cook 2 minutes, stir in egg.
5. Add green onions and sesame seed oil just before serving.

•

If prawns are not used, substitute more chopped or ground pork. If unable to find ground pork, use lean pork chops and mince the meat yourself. This soup reheats well. Add green onions just before serving.

Be sure to use unseasoned seaweed sheets. Some sheets are roasted and seasoned, used only in Japanese cooking in the making of sushi.

PORK AND SHRIMP SOUP
(4-6 servings)

4 C	soup stock
¼ C	black forest mushrooms (soaked and rinsed)
¼ C	bamboo shoots
¼ C	pork
½ C	raw shrimp (shelled, deveined and cut in half lengthwise)
¼ C	pea pods
½ C	tofu cut into ½ inch cubes
1	green onion cut in 1 inch diagonal pieces
1 T	rice wine

1. Slice mushrooms, bamboo shoots and pork in ⅛ inch thin strips, about 1½ inches in length.
2. Place soup stock into pan or heatproof casserole dish.
3. Add mushrooms, bamboo shoots and pork. Bring to a slow boil, turn temperature down and simmer 5 minutes.
4. Add shrimp, pea pods, and tofu. Cook 1 minute.
5. Add green onions and wine, remove from heat and serve.
6. Try to keep ingredients separate in the dish.

•

Easiest to cook and serve soup in the same casserole dish so ingredients are cooked without being disturbed.

Sake may be substituted for the rice wine.

BIRD'S NEST SOUP
(6-8 servings)

1 C	dried bird's nest
10 C	chicken stock
½ C	chopped lean pork
½ C	chopped chicken breast
¼ C	chopped water chestnuts
1 t	salt to taste
3 T	cornstarch dissolved in ¼ C water
¼ C	chopped ham

1. Soak nest until soft in hot water. Pick out impurities.

2. Rinse the bird's nest and add to soup stock, cover and simmer 2 hours.

3. Combine pork, chicken and water chestnuts in a bowl and mix in ½ C of stock to break apart the meat. Add to soup and stir to break apart meat.

4. Add salt to taste. Bring to boil and cook 5 minutes.

5. Thicken with cornstarch mixture, bringing soup to a full boil stirring constantly.

6. Garnish with chopped ham.

●

Soup may be completed through step 2 and refrigerated, or entire soup may be prepared and reheated.

Birds' nests are sold dried in a box, usually purchased in oriental stores.

There is no substitute. It has no taste of its own, therefore the flavor must come from the richness of the soup stock and other ingredients used.

SOUR AND HOT SOUP
(4-6 servings)

4 C	chicken stock
½ C	slivered pork
¼ C	slivered bamboo shoots
2	forest mushrooms (soaked, rinsed and sliced thin)
¼ C	cloud ears (2 T dried) soaked, rinsed and chopped
½	cube (1 cup) tofu sliced into thin strips
2 T	soy sauce
½ t	white pepper or to taste
3 T	rice vinegar
1	egg, beaten
2 T	cornstarch dissolved in 3 T water
¼ C	green onions chopped
2 T	preserved Szechuan vegetable chopped (optional)
1 t	sesame seed oil

1. Combine stock, pork, bamboo shoots, mushrooms and cloud ears. Bring to a boil and cook for 5 minutes, stirring to break up pork.

2. Add tofu and cook gently for 1 minute.

3. Add soy sauce, white pepper and rice vinegar.

4. Add egg and stir. Add cornstarch and water mixture, stir gently and bring to a slow boil.

5. Add green onions and preserved vegetable. Add sesame seed oil just before serving.

•

Soup may be prepared ahead and reheated gently. Be sure to rinse cloud ears well because it is sandy. Preserved Szechuan vegetable comes in cans. It is preserved with salt and chili pepper. Rinse before using. Keeps indefinitely in a jar with a tight lid, or freeze.

CORN SOUP
(6 servings)

1 C	chicken breast chopped fine
1	egg white
1 T	rice wine
1 T	cornstarch
4 C	chicken stock
1 C	creamed corn
1½ t	salt
½ t	white pepper
1	egg, beaten
2 T	cornstarch dissolved in 2 T water
1	green onion, chopped
¼ C	chopped ham (optional)

1. Combine chopped chicken breast, egg white, wine and cornstarch Set aside.
2. Combine soup stock, creamed corn, salt and white pepper. Bring to a boil, adding chicken mixture. Stir to break up chicken and cook one minute.
3. Add beaten egg in a thin stream and stir slowly in one direction.
4. Thicken with cornstarch and water mixture.
5. Garnish with green onions and ham.

•

½ cup of shredded cooked crab meat may be substituted for the ham and green onions.

SHRIMP AND EGG SOUP
(4-6 servings)

4 C   boiling water (to cook eggs)

4   eggs
½ t   salt

4 C   chicken stock
2 t   soy sauce
1 t   salt

6   prawns (shelled retaining tail and deveined)
6   pea pods
1   green onion cut on a bias

1 T   rice wine

1. Beat eggs with salt. Drop egg mixture into boiling water, stir and cook ½ minute. Pour contents into a strainer to drain off the water. Do not allow eggs to cool.

2. Place cooked eggs on a bamboo rolling mat and roll into a rod 1 inch in diameter. Allow to set 10 minutes before unrolling.

3. Unroll and cut into small ½ inch pieces. Set aside.

4. Slice prawns in half at the top end only. Set aside.

5. Bring soup stock to a boil, add soy sauce and salt.

6. Add prawns and vegetables. Bring to a boil and cook ½ minute.

7. Add the rice wine. Arrange egg pieces in a serving bowl and carefully pour in hot soup.

•

Use thin slices of chicken or fish instead of prawns. Use other green vegetables.

Bamboo rolling mats are used to make sushi in Japanese cooking and is called a maki su.

EGG FLOWER SOUP
(4-6 servings)

4 C   soup stock
1 ½ t   salt
½ C   green peas
½ C   sliced fresh mushrooms

½ t   cornstarch dissolved in 1 t water
2   eggs

1. Combine soup stock with salt, green peas, and mushrooms. Bring to a boil and cook 1 minute.
2. Combine cornstarch mixture with eggs and beat together.
3. Add egg mixture slowly to boilng soup and stir in one direction.

•

Any green vegetable may be substituted for the peas. Chopped cooked meats may also be added.

VEGETABLE SOUP
(4-6 servings)

4 C	soup stock
¼ C	diced pork
¼ C	diced onions
¼ C	diced celery
¼ C	green peas
¼ C	diced water chestnuts
½ C	diced tomatoes (skin removed)
1 ½ t	salt or to taste
1	egg beaten
1 t	sesame seed oil

1. Bring soup stock to a boil. Add pork, onions, celery, peas, water chestnuts and tomatoes. Bring soup to a boil and reduce temperature. Cover and cook 5 minutes.

2. Add salt to taste. Stir in egg and add sesame seed oil. Serve.

●

Cook tomatoes in boiling water for ½ minute, remove and skin will peel off easily. Other vegetables may also be used.

Add some hot sauce or pepper for a spicy taste.

The staple course served in any Chinese meal consists of either rice or noodles.

Rice & Noodle

STEAMED WHITE RICE

(yield 3 cups)   **(yield 4 cups)**

1 C   rice (long grain)   1 ½ C rice (short grain)
1 ½ C water   1 ¾ C water

1. Wash rice by rubbing between hands. (Some brands require no washing.) Drain and repeat until water is clear.

2. Add water, cover saucepan and bring to boil.

3. When rice comes to boil, uncover and allow rice to boil until (75%) or most of liquid evaporates and holes form on surface of rice. Cover rice, allow to steam on very low heat for 20 minutes.

4. Turn heat off and allow rice to sit 5 minutes on burner.

5. Fluff rice before serving.

●

Water proportion changes as more rice is used. If cooking more rice, add enough water to cover rice one inch or water level should be up to first joint of index finger. Increase or decrease water to the firmness desired.

When cooking short grain rice, use a little less water.

Left-over rice may be refrigerated. Reheat by steaming or use for fried rice.

●

Rice is an integral part of every meal, and is the staple food of China. Basically, there are three types: long grain, short grain, and glutinous, or sweet rice. Long grain rice is firmer, and is used for fried rice. Short grain is starchier and softer. Japanese sushi requires use of short grain rice. Sweet rice is usually used for desserts or stuffings.

FRIED RICE I
(long grain)
(4 servings)

3 T	oil
2	eggs, beaten
3	strips bacon cut into 1 inch pieces
½ C	cooked meat diced (pork, chicken, shrimp or ham)
1	small onion diced
1 C	beansprouts
3 C	cooked long grain rice
2-3 T	soy sauce
1	green onion chopped

1. Heat 1 T oil in the wok and scramble eggs. Remove and set aside.
2. Fry bacon in the wok until most of the fat is cooked out. Drain off excess fat and replace with 2 T oil.
3. Add cooked meat, onions and beansprouts. Stir fry about 1 minute.
4. Add rice and soy sauce. Fry until rice is hot, turning temperature down if necessary.
5. Add eggs and mix in with rice. Toss in green onions.

•

Other meats and vegetables may be used to produce a variety of fried rice recipes.

Chinese sausage can be added to recipe. Cut in small pieces and cook with the bacon.

FRIED RICE II
(short grain)
(4 servings)

½ C   bacon cut in small pieces
½ C   Chinese sausage cut in small pieces

½ C   chopped onions
½ C   chopped celery
½ C   sliced fresh mushrooms

4 C   cooked short grain rice (one recipe of white rice, short grain)

2 T   soy sauce
1 T   oyster sauce

¼ C   chopped green onions

1. Fry bacon and sausage in the wok. Drain off excess fat.
2. Add onions, celery and mushrooms. Cook 1 minute.
3. Mix in rice. Stir fry until rice is hot, turning down temperature.
4. Add soy sauce and oyster sauce. Blend thoroughly.
5. Toss in chopped green onions.

•

Other meats and vegetables may be used.
This recipe is delicious as a stuffing for chicken or cornish hens.

PAN FRIED NOODLES

1. In a large pot, bring some water to a full boil.
2. Cook desired amount of noodles in boiling water until tender.
3. Remove noodles from pot, rinse with cold water and drain thoroughly.

To Pan Fry Noodles

1. Heat a frying pan (preferably non-stick) on medium high heat. Add about 2 tablespoons of oil and cook noodles in a one inch layer until golden brown. Turn noodles over and brown other side, adding more oil if necessary. Remove and set aside.
2. Any cooked meat or vegetable dish may be served over the noodles or the noodles may be mixed in with the meat or vegetable dish.

•

Depending on the type of noodles used, the boiling time will vary. Thin noodles will take less time, about 2 minutes, while thick noodles will take 6 to 10 minutes or cook until tender. Follow package instructions if available. Steamed Chinese noodles should be pan fried without boiling first.
Use about one half pound of steamed noodles for each recipe of chow mein. Most recipes call for about one half pound of **cooked** noodles.
Some noodles expand more during cooking than others. Use enough dried noodles to get one half pound after cooking.

RICE NOODLES
(Fun)
(5-6 rolls)

1 C	cake flour (sifted)
1 T	cornstarch
½ t	salt
1 T	oil
1¼ C	water

1. Combine all ingredients in order and beat until smooth. If there are too many lumps, strain mixture.

2. Bring some water to a full steam in the wok. Oil a 9 inch round cake pan.

3. Pour in enough batter to cover the bottom of the pan ⅛ inch deep. (⅓ C).

4. Place on top of steaming rack in the wok and steam for 5 minutes at full steam.

5. Remove pan and allow to cool by floating the pan in some cold water.

6. Roll up sheet of noodle like a jelly roll. Set aside.

7. Repeat until all batter is used. Check water level in wok constantly, adding more water as needed.

8. Slice the jelly rolls into ¾ inch pieces and use as a noodle.
   A selection of meat and vegetable dishes can be served with the fun noodles, producing a dish similar to chow mein.

•

Use two pans to steam batter; one can be steaming while the other is cooling.

Noodles can be made ahead, covered and stored in the refrigerator.

Wash pans between steaming if noodles are hard to remove. Cake pans with the non-stick coating work very well.

CHOW FUN
(rice noodles with vegetables)
(4 servings)

1	recipe of rice noodles (Fun noodles) (pg. 84)
6 T	oil
½ lb	beef sliced thin against the grain
1 t	sugar
2 t	soy sauce
2 t	cornstarch
1	small onion, sliced
1	stalk celery, sliced
1	large forest mushroom (soaked, rinsed and sliced)
2 C	Chinese greens (bok choy) sliced ½ inch diagonally
¼ C	sliced bamboo shoots
¼ C	sliced water chestnuts
1 t	salt
1 T	oyster sauce
1 T	rice wine
1 C	soup stock
	cornstarch for thickening

1. Heat 2 T oil ina skillet and slowly fry fun noodles until hot. Set aside.
2. Combine beef with sugar, soy sauce and cornstarch.
3. Heat 2 T oil in the wok, cook beef, remove and set aside.
4. Heat 2 T oil in wok, add all vegetables, salt, oyster sauce, wine and soup stock. Cover, bring to boil, cook ½ minutes.
5. Thicken with cornstarch dissolved in water to form a medium thick gravy.
6. Pour over fun noodles. Noodles can also be combined with vegetables in wok.

●

Non-stick skillets are best for frying noodles.

Other vegetables and meats can be used such as prawns, chicken, pork, peapods and other fancy vegetables. When using other meats, do not combine with soy sauce, and decrease the sugar to ½ teaspoon. Remove only prawns and chicken, leaving pork to cook with the vegetables in the wok.

PORK CHOW MEIN
(4 servings)

8 oz	soft chow mein noodles (steamed Chinese noodles)
3 T	oil
2 T	oil
½ lb	pork, sliced thin
1	small onion, sliced
3	forest mushrooms (soaked, rinsed and sliced)
¼ C	sliced water chestnuts
¼ C	sliced bamboo shoots
1	stalk celery, sliced
1 C	bean sprouts
½ C	pea pods
1 T	mirin
1 t	salt
1 C	soup stock
1	green onion cut in one inch pieces
1 T	cornstarch dissolved in 1 T water

1. Brown the noodles in 3 T oil on medium high heat, remove and set aside.
2. Add the 2 T oil to wok and cook pork on high heat until no longer pink. (2 minutes).
3. Add all other ingredients except green onions and cornstarch mixture.
4. Cover and bring to full boil, allow to steam one minute.
5. Toss in green onions and stir in cornstarch mixture to thicken.
6. Add noodles to vegetable mixture and toss to combine.

●

If unable to obtain soft Chinese noodles, sometimes called steamed Chinese noodles, substitute dried noodles. Dried noodles must be boiled according to package instructions, rinsed and drained, then fry in oil until brown.
Pea pods may be subtituted; use green pepper, bok choy, or thin sliced carrots. Other meats may be used such as chicken, shrimp, beef, barbecued pork or ham.

TOMATO BEEF CHOW MEIN
(4 servings)

1	recipe pan fried noodles (pg. 83)
2 T	oil
¼ lb	beef, sliced ⅛ inch thick against the grain
2 t	soy sauce
2 t	cornstarch
1 t	sugar
1	small onion wedged
1	small green pepper wedged
3	tomatoes cut into wedges

Sauce

1 C	water
1 T	cornstarch
¼ C	catsup
½ t	salt
2 T	sugar

1. Prepare 1 recipe of pan fried noodles. Set aside.
2. Combine beef slices with soy sauce, cornstarch and sugar. Combine sauce ingredients.
3. Heat wok and add the oil. Stir fry the beef until done, remove and set aside.
4. Add onions and peppers to wok, stir fry a few seconds to break apart onions.
5. Add sauce mixture, bring to a full boil to thicken.
6. Add tomato wedges and beef. Stir gently to combine. Mix in noodles.

●

Add about one teaspoon of curry powder when stir frying the onions and green peppers to make curry beef tomato chow mein.

OYSTER SAUCE BEEF NOODLES
(4 servings)

½ lb   Chinese noodles

2 T   oil
½ lb   flank steak
1 C   sliced fresh mushrooms
¼ C   oyster sauce
½ C   water or soup stock
2   green onions cut into 1 inch pieces

cornstarch for thickening

1. Bring some water to a boil and cook noodles until tender. Rinse, drain and place on a platter.
2. Slice steak into ¼ inch thick slices against the grain.
3. Heat oil in wok until hot, add beef and cook until amost done.
4. Push beef aside and add the sliced mushrooms, stir fry for a few seconds.
5. Add oyster sauce and water, bring to a boil, add green onions and thicken with cornstarch and water.
6. Serve over the noodles.

●

Add any other green vegetable that cooks fast such as peapods or bok choy.

BEEF W/ PEAS & NOODLES
(4 servings)

½ lb	Chinese noodles boiled, rinsed and drained
2 T	oil
½ lb	ground beef or sliced beef
½ C	green peas
4 T	oyster sauce
1	green onion, chopped

1. Heat oil in wok and cook beef until done. Add peas and cook ½ minute.
2. Add noodles and oyster sauce, cook until hot, turning temperature down if necessary.
3. Garnish with green onions.

●

If using ground beef, be sure to drain off excess oil before adding the green peas.

BARBECUED PORK NOODLES
(2 servings)

¼ lb	Chinese noodles
3 T	chicken stock
1 t	salt or to taste
12	slices cooked barbecued pork
2	hard boiled eggs cut into halves
1	green onion chopped

1. Cook noodles in boiling water until tender. Rinse, drain and place in 2 individual servings bowls.
2. Bring soup stock to a boil, adding salt. Pour over noodles and garnish with pork slices and egg halves. Top with chopped green onions.

•

Barbecued spareribs or chicken may also be used. Try this recipe served with sesame seed oil and soy sauce.

WOR MEIN
(2 servings)

¼ lb   Chinese noodles

4 C   soup stock
1½ t   salt or to taste
8   prawns shelled, deveined and cut in half lengthwise
2   medium forest mushrooms (soaked, rinsed and sliced)
4   water chestnuts sliced
2   Chinese sausages sliced in ¼ inch thick diagonal slices
2 C   sliced green vegetables such as bok choy (Chinese greens)

1   green onion, chopped
2   hard boiled eggs, cut in halves

1. Boil noodles until tender. Rinse, drain and set aside in a large serving bowl.

2. Bring soup stock to a boil, adding salt, meats and vegetables. Cook gently for 2 minutes.

3. Add green onions and pour all ingredients over noodles.

4. Arrange egg halves on top and serve.

•

Whatever ingredients on hand may be used such as scallops, squid, liver or chicken sliced thin.

Vary the vegetables by using peapods or nappa or spinach.

SEAFOOD CHOW MEIN
(4 servings)

1	recipe of pan fried noodles (pg. 83)
3 T	oil
1	clove garlic minced
½ lb	prawns (shelled, deveined and rinsed)
¼ lb	scallops
¼ t	salt
1 t	wine
½	egg white
1 T	cornstarch
1	small onion, wedged
¼ lb	pea pods
1 C	bok choy leaves (use the hearts of the bok choy if available)
¼ C	sliced water chestnuts
⅓ C	sliced bamboo shoots
2	large forest mushrooms (soaked, rinsed and sliced ¼" thick)
¾ C	soup stock
1 T	oyster sauce
½ t	salt or to taste
	cornstarch and water for thickening

1. Prepare one recipe of pan fried noodles according to instructions. Place on a large platter.
2. Cut prawns in half lengthwise. Slice scallops into ¼ inch thick slices. Combine with salt, wine, egg white and cornstarch. Set aside.
3. Prepare all other ingredients.
4. Heat wok and add 2 T oil and garlic. Stir fry prawns and scallops until done. (2 minutes) Remove from wok and set aside.
5. Add 1 T to wok, add all vegetables and stir fry a few seconds. Add soup stock, oyster sauce and salt. Cover, bring to a boil and cook ½ minute.
6. Add seafood to vegetables, thicken with cornstarch mixture and gently stir to combine. Pour ingredients over pan fried noodles or mix noodles with the ingredients in the wok.

●

Other vegetables may be used. Use ¾ lb. chicken instead of seafood. Slice the chicken ¼ inch thick and follow recipe exactly. Try this recipe with fun noodles, pg. 84.

MAIFUN WITH CHICKEN
(4 servings)

6½ oz. maifun (rice sticks)

3 T. oil

2 eggs, beaten

1 C shredded chicken breast

½ C sliced onions
1 C sliced fresh mushrooms
½ C slivered carrots
1 C shredded cabbage
¼ C soy sauce
½ t salt
1 C soup stock

1. Soak maifun in hot water until soft (10 minutes). Drain water and cut into shorter lengths. Set aside.
2. Heat wok and add 1 T oil. Scramble eggs in wok, remove and set aside.
3. Add 2 T oil to wok and stir fry chicken until done. (2 minutes)
4. Add onions, mushrooms, carrots, cabbage, soy sauce, salt and soup stock.
5. Bring mixture to a full boil and add maifun. Cook until maifun is tender or liquid is gone. Mix in eggs.

Other meats or vegetables may be used.
Purita, this recipe is for you!

MANDARIN PANCAKES
(24 pancakes)

2 C   all purpose flour
¾ C   boiling water
1-2 T   sesame seed oil

1. Place flour in a large bowl, make a well in the center of flour and pour in hot water.
2. Stir with chopsticks until a dough is formed. Knead on a lightly floured surface until smooth. (10 minutes)
3. Cover dough and let rest for 15 minutes.
4. On a lightly floured surface, roll out dough ¼ inch thick. Cut 2½ inch circles. Continue until all dough is used.
5. Brush half of the circles with oil and stack by two's, like a sandwich.
6. Roll out each pair of circles in a clockwise direction, forming a six inch circle.
7. Heat a heavy ungreased skillet to 375°. Cook pancakes for 1 minute, turning over once. (Brown specks are common)
8. While pancakes are still warm, separate halves and stack. Place in a covered dish to keep warm.
9. To serve, fold each pancake into fourths and arrange on a platter.

Mandarin pancakes may be served as a wrapper for:

1. Mu shu pork
2. Chicken with scrambled eggs
3. Shrimp with green peas
4. Beansprouts with pork

Sauces to spread on the wrappers are: Hoisin sauce, plum sauce, hot mustard or any kind of hot sauce.

●

If making wrappers ahead, wrap in foil and freeze. To reheat, allow wrappers to defrost in the foil. Place in a warm oven to reheat. Pancakes may also be steamed to reheat.

Meat dishes such as beef, pork and chicken may be combined with vegetables, but will also often be found standing alone as a main course. The meat is usually shredded, sliced, or cubed into succulent bite-sized pieces for convenient serving.

Meat & Poultry

BASIC SAUCE

Basic Sauce

2 C	soy sauce (Kikkoman)
½ C	dark or thick soy sauce
2 C	water
¼ C	rice wine
¼ C	sugar
3	cloves garlic
3	whole star anise (1 T)
3	large slices ginger root
4	dried chili peppers
¼ C	peanut oil

1. Combine all ingredients of the sauce, bring to a boil, turn down to simmer and cook sauce for 10 minutes. Now sauce is ready to be used to cook whatever meat or vegetable desired.

The flavor of the sauce improves with time and the sauce can be used over and over for months. As the sauce is used, more soy sauce or some of the other ingredients may need to be replenished to keep the proper balance of flavors.

•

The sauce should be covered and stored in the refrigerator or freezer after each use. After the sauce has been used several times, remove the layer of fat on the surface and replace with ¼ cup fresh oil.

BASIC SAUCE MEATS
OR VEGETABLES

Always bring basic sauce to a full boil, drop in food to be cooked, and then turn the temperature down to simmer. Cover the pot and simmer until done.

Whole chicken — 3 lbs. — or Cornish Hens

1. Simmer whole chicken in sauce for 20 minutes. Turn chicken over and simmer 20 minutes more.
2. Remove from sauce, brush entire chicken with vegetable oil, and allow to cool for 10 minutes.
3. Cut chicken into bite size pieces and arrange on platter.

Chicken legs or thighs

1. Simmer for 25 minutes.

Chicken wings

1. Cut wings into separate parts discarding tips. Simmer for 15 minutes.

Gizzards and livers

1. Simmer for 15 minutes.

Eggs

1. Cook eggs in water as for hard boiled eggs. Cool eggs in cold water and peel.
2. Simmer eggs in sauce for 45 minutes. Slice in wedges and serve. Also good cold.

Bean Curd or tofu

1. Cut bean curd into desired size cubes. Bring sauce to a boil, drop in bean curb, turn off heat and allow to steep for 10 minutes.

●

Other meats and vegetables may be used.

BON BON CHICKEN
(4 servings)

2   whole chicken breasts or one whole fryer (3 lbs.)

2 T   vegetable oil

Sauce I

½ C   soup stock
1 T   minced ginger root
2   cloves garlic, minced
½ t   sugar
2 T   soy sauce

1 t   hot sesame seed oil

1   cucumber
1 t   salt

Sauce II

2 T   rice vinegar
1 T   mirin
1 T   sugar

1. Cover chicken with water and bring to a boil. Simmer for ½ hour and turn off heat. Allow chicken to poach in the pot until done (15 minutes). A whole chicken will take a total of 45 minutes. Remove from pot, brush chicken with oil and allow to cool.

2. Combine soup stock, ginger root, garlic, sugar and soy sauce in a pot. Bring to a boil and reduce by half. Allow sauce to cool and add hot sesame seed oil.

3. Cut cucumber and remove seeds. Slice thin and sprinkle with salt. Allow to sit 5 minutes, rinse and drain.

4. Combine rice vinegar, mirin and sugar. Pour over cucumbers. Set aside.

5. Remove bones from chicken and cut into bite size pieces. Arrange on a platter and garnish with cucumber slices. Serve Sauce I as a dip or pour over chicken pieces.

●

Poached Chicken may also be served plain with oyster sauce as a dip.

STEAMED CHICKEN WITH MUSHROOMS AND TIGER LILY BUDS
(4 servings)

¾ lb	or 1 ½ C boneless chicken sliced ½ inch thick
1	Chinese sausage sliced thin, diagonally
3	large forest mushrooms
25	dried tiger lily buds
1 T	soy sauce
1 t	rice wine
½ t	salt
1 T	cornstarch

1. Soak mushrooms and tiger lily buds in hot water until soft. Rinse, cut off stems of mushrooms and slice thin. Cut off hard stems of bud and cut buds into 1 inch pieces.

2. Combine all ingredients well and place in a heatproof plate with a rim.

3. Place in a steamer, bring to a full steam and turn down to medium high. Steam 20 minutes or until done. Serve in steaming dish.

●

Vary this recipe with pork, fresh mushrooms, carrots sliced thin, or combine pork with chicken. Also chicken with bone may be used, such as chicken wings or thighs cut in half. Allow longer steaming time for larger pieces of meat. Spareribs are also good. Cut into 1 ½ inch pieces as for sweet and sour spareribs.

FOIL WRAPPED CHICKEN
(4 servings)

24	5" x 5" pieces of foil
2	chicken breasts, boned and cut in bitesize pieces. 2"x1"x½" (about 24 pieces)

Marinade:

¼ C	soy sauce
2 T	mirin
2 T	sugar
1	clove garlic, crushed
2	slices ginger root, crushed
2	Chinese sausages, sliced or 24 pieces of ham
5	fresh mushrooms, sliced
2	green onions, cut into 1½ inch pieces
2	inches oil for deep frying (375°)

1. Marinate chicken in sauce for ½ hour.
2. Place on foil a piece of chicken, sausage, mushroom and some green onions. Wrap according to instructions.
3. Fry in oil (375°) for approximately 3 minutes, turning once or twice.

To wrap:

1. Fold bottom of foil up to cover ingredients.
2. Bring sides in to overlap.
3. Fold up and tuck top into fold.

Wrap chicken ahead and keep in refrigerator. Deep fry and keep warm in oven. Try other meats or seafoods and try different combinations. Marinate fresh meats only.

SWEET AND SOUR CHICKEN
(4-6 servings)

2	chicken breasts, boned and cut into ½ inch thick slices
1 t	salt

Batter

½ C	flour
¼ C	cornstarch
1 t	baking powder
½ t	baking soda
¾ C	cold water

Sweet and Sour Sauce

¾ C	water
2 T	cornstarch
2 T	rice vinegar
3 T	catsup
⅔ C	sugar

Garnish

1	tomato, wedged
1	small green pepper, wedged
½ C	pineapple chunks
1 t	toasted sesame seeds

3 C	oil for deep frying (375°)

1. Heat oil in wok to 375°.

2. Rub salt into chicken pieces. Dip into batter and deep fry in oil until golden brown. (About 4 minutes)

3. Bring sauce to a full boil stirring constantly.

4. Arrange tomato, pepper and pineapple chunks on top of chicken, pour sauce over and sprinkle sesame seeds on top.

●

Try other meats or seafoods. Be sure meat is dry before dipping into batter. Unused batter should be covered and stored in the refrigerator. Use the next day. The vegetables may be cooked in the sauce to warm.

Do not serve this dish with tomato beef, tomato sauce prawns or spicy prawns.

ALMOND BREADED CHICKEN
(4-6 servings)

2	whole chicken breasts
½ t	salt

½ C	all purpose flour
1	egg, beaten
1 C	panko (dehydrated bread crumb)
¼ C	sliced almonds

3 C	oil for deep frying (375°)

Gravy

1¼ C	chicken stock
2 T	cornstarch
1 t	mirin
1 T	soy sauce

outer edge

2 C	shredded lettuce

¼ C	toasted, slivered almonds

1. Remove bones and skin from chicken breast.
2. Cut each whole chicken breast into halves at the center.
3. **Butterfly** each half by slicing breast from the outer edge, part way through, to open like a book. (The halves will resemble a whole breast, but thinner. This is to enable faster cooking.)
4. Sprinkle ½ t salt over chicken breasts.
5. Combine panko with sliced almonds.
6. Coat each piece of chicken with flour, dip in egg and press on panko mixture.
7. Fry in hot oil (375°) for 4 minutes or until golden brown.
8. Cut chicken into bite-size pieces and place on top of a bed of shredded lettuce.
9. Bring gravy to a full boil stirring constantly. Pour over chicken and top with toasted slivered almonds. Serve immediately.

●

Kimmie's favorite.

To keep chicken crisp, serve gravy in a separate dish.
Almonds can be toasted in the oven at 375° for 10 minutes. Chicken pieces can be breaded ahead and refrigerated. Chicken thighs or legs can be used instead of breasts.

STUFFED BONELESS CHICKEN
(4 servings)

1	large whole chicken breast, boned and skinned
1 t	minced ginger root
1 t	rice wine
½ t	salt and dash of black pepper

Filling Ingredients

¼ C	chopped prawns (shelled and deveined)
¼ C	chopped pork
¼ C	chopped fresh mushrooms
2 T	chopped bamboo shoots
1	green onion, chopped
1 t	minced ginger root
½ t	salt
1 T	cornstarch
½	egg white

½ C	all purpose flour
1	egg, beaten
1 C	panko (dehydrated bread crumbs)

3 C	oil for deep frying (375°)

2 C	shredded lettuce

1. Lay chicken breast flat and cut into halves. Gently pound with blunt edge of cleaver.
2. Rub each half with ginger, wine, salt and pepper.
3. Combine all filling ingredients and press onto top of chicken pieces.
4. Gently coat each piece with flour, egg and press on panko.
5. Deep fry in 375° oil for 5-6 minutes, turning to brown evenly.
6. Cut chicken into bite-size pieces and serve on top of shredded lettuce.

●

Wet fingers to smooth top of filling over chicken pieces.

ALMOND BREADED CHICKEN WINGS
(4-6 servings)

2 lbs.   chicken wings

1 t   salt
½ t   pepper
½ t   garlic powder

½ C   all purpose flour
2   eggs, beaten
2 C   panko (dehydrated bread crumbs)
½ C   sliced almonds

3 C   oil for deep frying (375°)

1. Separate chicken wings at joints, discarding tips.
2. Rub with salt, pepper and garlic powder.
3. Combine sliced almonds with panko.
4. Dust wings with all purpose flour, roll in egg and press on panko.
5. Deep fry at 375° for 8 minutes or until golden brown.

•

Panko is a dehydrated bread crumb. Purchase at Uwajimaya or major grocery store.

Use other chicken parts, adjusting frying time.

Try this recipe with fish or prawns.

MINIATURE DRUM STICKS
(4-6 servings)

2 lbs.   chicken wings

1 t   salt

Batter		**Sweet and Sour Dip**	
½ C	all purpose flour	¾ C	cold water
¼ C	cornstarch	2 T	cornstarch
1 t	baking powder	2 T	rice vinegar
½ t	baking soda	3 T	catsup
¾ C	cold water	⅔ C	sugar

3 C   oil for deep frying (375°)

1. Separate wings at joints, discard tips.
2. The larger piece has one bone; remove the meat from the smaller end and push meat up, forming a small drumstick.
3. The flat piece has two bones. Remove the smaller of the two bones. Release the meat from one end and push meat up, forming a small drumstick. Repeat process with other wings.
4. Sprinkle salt over chicken pieces. Combine batter ingredients.
5. Heat oil in wok to 375°. Dip each piece into batter (meat only) and deep fry for 5 minutes or until done.
6. Bring sauce to a full boil, stirring constantly. Serve as a dip for miniature drumsticks.

CHINESE STYLE FRIED CHICKEN
(4 servings)

1	fryer chicken (approx. 3 lbs.)
1 T	rice wine
1	clove garlic, minced
1 t	ginger root, minced
½ t	salt
½ t	sugar
½ t	five spice powder
1 T	soy sauce
oil	for deep frying (375°)

1. Rinse chicken and dry with paper towels.
2. Place chicken in a large bowl and rub ingredients on chicken in order.
3. Allow to marinate for at least 2 hours.
4. Heat about 4 cups of oil in the wok to 375°.
5. Carefully place chicken in wok, breast side down first. Fry chicken for approximately ½ hour, turning often to allow for even browning.
6. Remove from oil and allow to cool 15 minutes before cutting into bite size pieces.

•

A 14-inch wok is best for deep frying, allowing more depth for the oil and chicken.

Be sure oil is not too hot; adjust temperature to maintain about 375°.

Chicken can also be baked in the oven at 375° for approximately 1 hour and 10 minutes.

FU YU FRIED CHICKEN
(4 servings)

1	3 lb. fryer cut into small 3 inch pieces
½ t	salt
½ t	sugar
1	clove garlic, minced
1 t	minced ginger root
2 T	fu yu (fermented white bean curd)

Batter

¼ C	all purpose flour
2 T	cornstarch
½ t	baking powder
⅛ t	baking soda
⅓ C	water

½ C	all purpose flour
3 C	oil for deep frying (375°)

1. Combine chicken pieces with salt, sugar, garlic, ginger and fu yu. Allow to marinate for about one half hour or longer.
2. Mix together the batter and pour over chicken pieces. Turn mixture to coat each piece of chicken.
3. Pour in ½ C all purpose flour to gently dust each piece of chicken.
4. Heat 3 cups of oil in the wok to 375°. Drop in several pieces of chicken and deep fry 12 to 15 minutes or until done. Turn pieces as needed to brown evenly.

●

Fu yu is a fermented white bean curd with a cheesy flavor. It is sold bottled in half-inch thick rectangles. Keeps in refrigerator indefinitely after opening.

HOT SPICED CHICKEN
(4 servings)

1 ½ lbs chicken thighs cut in half

Coat chicken with:

½ t	hot pepper
2 t	sesame seed oil
1 T	soy sauce
½ t	salt
½ t	sugar
1 t	rice wine
2 t	minced ginger root
1	clove garlic, minced
1	egg yolk
¼ C	cornstarch
3 C	oil for deep frying (375°)

Sauce for spicy fried chicken (optional)

2 T	soy sauce
1 T	sugar
2 t	sesame seed oil
1	clove garlic, minced
1 t	minced ginger root
½ t	hot soy bean paste or chili paste with garlic
1	green onion, chopped

Gently heat sauce until warm. Pour over pieces of spicy fried chicken.

1. Coat chicken pieces and set aside for ½ hour.
2. Add egg yolk and cornstarch to chicken pieces and mix thoroughly.
3. Deep fry in hot oil for 5 minutes. Remove chicken from oil; allow oil to heat back up to 375° and refry chicken for 3 more minutes.
4. Serve with sauce if desired.

FIVE SPICE FRIED CHICKEN
(4-6 servings)

2½ lb   fryer cut up into small 2 inch pieces
1½ t   salt
1 T   rice wine
2 t   soy sauce
1   clove garlic, minced
1 t   minced ginger root
1½ t   five spice powder

½ C   all purpose flour

3 C   oil for deep frying (375°)

1. Rub chicken with salt, wine, soy sauce, garlic, ginger root, and five spice powder. Allow to marinate for 2 hours in the refrigerator.

2. Coat chicken pieces with flour.

3. Fry chicken for 12-15 minutes or until done.

CHICKEN WITH SOY SAUCE GLAZE
(4-6 servings)

1	3 lb. fryer (cut up into pieces about the size of thighs)
2 T	oil
1	clove garlic, minced

Sauce

¼ C	soy sauce
¼ C	mirin
¼ C	water

cornstarch and water for thickening (if needed)

1	green onion, chopped

1. Brown chicken in oil on high heat, adding the garlic. (5 minutes) Drain off excess fat.

2. Add sauce, cover and simmer 20 minutes. Turn chicken pieces over once, while simmering.

3. Thicken with cornstarch and water if needed or allow sauce to cook down, forming a glaze.

4. Toss green onions on top of chicken.

•

Chicken parts such as thighs may be substituted.

CHICKEN WITH OYSTER SAUCE
(4-6 servings)

2 lbs	chicken wings or thighs
1 T	soy sauce
1	clove garlic, minced
1 t	minced ginger root
2 T	oil
3 T	oyster sauce
1 T	mirin
½ t	salt
1 C	water
2 t	sesame seed oil
	cornstarch and water for thickening
1	bunch spinach, blanched

1. Cut chicken wings into individual parts, discarding tips. If using thighs, cut in half.
2. Combine chicken pieces with soy sauce, garlic and ginger. Set aside for ½ hour.
3. Heat wok and add oil. Lightly brown chicken on high heat, drain excess oil from wok.
4. Add oyster sauce, mirin, salt and water. Cover, bring to boil and turn temperature down. Cook 15 to 20 minutes.
5. Turn temperature to high, add sesame seed oil, thicken with cornstarch to make a medium thick gravy.
6. Arrange the blanched spinach on a platter and serve chicken pieces on top.

BRAISED COCONUT CHICKEN
(4-6 servings)

2 lbs chicken parts (thighs or wings)

1 T oil

2 cloves garlic, minced

2 T coconut syrup
2 T rice vinegar
1 ¼ C water
1 T soy sauce
1 t salt

1 lemon, sliced

1. Heat wok, add oil and garlic. Add chicken and saute on high heat until light brown. Drain excess oil from wok.
2. Add coconut syrup, vinegar, water, soy sauce and salt. Cover and simmer for 20 minutes, stirring once or twice.
3. Remove the cover. Turn heat to high and allow some of the liquid to cook away, forming a glaze.
4. Garnish chicken with slices of fresh lemon.

BROILED CHICKEN WINGS
(4-6 servings)

2 lbs   chicken wings

Sauce

½ C   soy sauce
¼ C   mirin
1   clove garlic, minced
1 t   minced ginger root
1 T   sugar

1. Separate wings at joints, discard tips.
2. Marinate wings in sauce for 2 hours.
3. Charcoal broil or oven broil, turning as needed (20-25 minutes).

●

Place chicken 6 inches from the broiler. Chicken may also be baked until done. Other chicken parts may be used. Adjust marinating and cooking time.

HOISIN SAUCE CHICKEN
(4 servings)

1 ½	lbs chicken parts such as wings or thighs
2 T	oil
1	clove garlic, crushed
2 T	hoisin sauce
½ t	salt
½ C	water or soup stock
1	green onion, chopped

1. Separate wings at joints, discard tips. If using thighs, chop in half.
2. Heat oil in wok and brown meat on all sides, turning temperature down if too hot. (10 minutes.)
3. Add crushed garlic and fry ½ minute.
4. Drain off excess fat. Add hoisin sauce, salt and water. Cover, bring to a boil and cook until most of liquid has evaporated (about 5 minutes). Reduce temperature if liquid is cooking off too fast.
5. Garnish with green onions and serve hot.

•

Boneless chicken may be used. Reduce browning time. Spareribs are also good. Use 1 ½ inch pieces as for sweet and sours.

HOISIN SAUCE BAKED CHICKEN
(4 servings)

2 lbs chicken parts (legs or thighs)

Sauce

½ C   hoisin sauce
¼ C   ketchup
½ t   five spice powder
1   clove garlic, minced
2 T   sugar
2 T   mirin

1. Combine sauce ingredients.
2. Spread sauce over chicken pieces and bake in the oven at 350°
   for 45 minutes. Turn and baste chicken once or twice as needed.
   Serve hot.

●

Other meats may be used such as pork spareribs or beef short ribs.
Bake other meats in the same manner until done.

FIVE SPICE BAKED CHICKEN
(4-6 servings)

2½ lb fryer cut up into small 2 inch pieces
1½ t   salt
1 T   rice wine
2 t   soy sauce
1   clove garlic, minced
1 t   minced ginger root
1½ t   five spice powder

1. Rub chicken with salt, wine, soy sauce, garlic, ginger root, and
   five spice powder. Allow to marinate for 2 hours.
2. Bake chicken pieces at 350° for 45 minutes.

STUFFED CORNISH HENS
(6-8 servings)

6	Cornish hens or 2 frying chickens
2 T	oil
¼ C	chopped shrimp, pork or chicken
½ C	chopped onions
½ C	bean sprouts
3	forest mushrooms (soaked, rinsed and chopped)
2 T	soy sauce
½ t	salt
2 C	cooked long grain rice
¼ C	melted butter

1. Clean hens and wipe dry.
2. Heat wok, add oil and cook meat until done (about 2 minutes).
3. Add onions, bean sprouts and mushrooms. Cook 1 minute.
4. Add soy sauce and salt. Mix in rice and continue to cook 1 minute.
5. Stuff hens with rice mixture. Close cavities of hens and brush with butter.
6. Roast hens at 350° for approximately 1 hour and 15 minutes. Baste with butter and turn hens every ½ hour.
7. May be served whole or cut in half.

ORIENTAL STUFFING

2 T	oil
¾ C	diced onions
¾ C	diced celery
¾ C	chopped bamboo shoots
½ C	chopped water chestnuts
3	forest mushrooms (soaked, rinsed and diced)

1 ½ C	soup stock
2 T	soy sauce
2 T	rice wine

1 ½ C	diced, cooked barbecued pork

1	7 ½ oz. package of seasoned stuffing mix

1. Heat wok, add oil and cook onions and celery for one minute. Add bamboo shoots, water chestnuts and mushrooms. Cook one minute.
2. Add soup stock, soy sauce and wine. Turn off heat and toss in barbecued pork and stuffing mix.
3. Stuff fowl and roast as usual.
4. Enough stuffing for a 10 lb. fowl. Roast in oven at 350° for about 2 ½ hours or until done. Baste with butter as needed.

●

This stuffing is also very good for chicken or Cornish hens as well as turkey.

ROAST DUCK
(4 servings)

1	4-5 lb. duck
½ C	catsup
½ C	vinegar
¼ C	honey
2½ C	water
1 T	brown bean sauce
2 t	hoisin sauce
1	clove garlic, minced
1 t	minced ginger root
2 t	sugar
20	green onion brushes
20	mandarin pancakes (1 recipe) pg. 94
½ C	hoisin sauce

1. Clean duck and pat dry inside and out. Cut off wing tips and discard.
2. In a large pot, bring catsup, vinegar, honey and water to a full boil.
3. Holding duck over the pot, baste with the sauce until the skin becomes tight. Discard sauce.
4. Hang and dry duck by using an electric fan. It should take about ½ hour.
5. Combine bean sauce, hoisin sauce, garlic, ginger root and sugar. Carefully rub the inside only of the dry duck and close the opening.
6. Place duck on a rack in the oven over a pan of water and roast at 375° for one hour. Then increase temperature to 425° and roast another 15 minutes or until done. Turn duck every half hour or as needed.

7. Make green onions brushes by cutting the white part of the green onions into 2 inch pieces. Cut each end of the onion tips to resemble a broom. Place in ice water, in the refrigerator, for one hour to allow brushes to curl. Drain.

8. Allow duck to cool for 20 minutes. Slice meat into ½ inch thick slices, arrange on platter, garnished with green onion brushes.

9. Have pancakes on a plate to follow the duck. Use hoisin sauce as a dip.

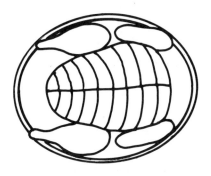

To serve:

Take a green onion brush, dip into hoisin sauce, brush onto the pancake and place a piece of duck inside with the green onion. Roll everything up and eat.

My Grandfather's recipe.

BARBECUED PORK I.
(Char Siu)

2½-3 lbs boneless pork (pork loin or tenderloin) cut into 2½x2x7
inch pieces

Marinade

1½ t	salt
1 T	rice wine
½ t	garlic powder
2 T	hoisin sauce
¼ C	catsup
¼ C	sugar
3	drops red food coloring (optional)
	paper clips to hang pork strips

1. Cut pork into strips 2½x2x7 inches. Some pieces may vary in length.

2. Marinate pork strips at least 2 hours or overnight in the refrigerator.

3. Separate both racks of oven as far apart as possible to hang the
   pork strips.

4. Unwind paper clips to form hooks. Hook each strip of pork in
   the center, and hang from the top rack of the oven over a pan of
   water in the lower rack.

5. Roast at 350° for 1 hour or until done.

6. Allow to cool. Slice into ¼" slices. Serve with hot mustard, toasted
   sesame seeds and hot catsup.

Pork strips may also be roasted on a rack over a pan of water
without hanging. Be sure to turn pork at least once.

•

Hot mustard is purchased as a powder. To prepare, combine 1 T mustard
to 1 T water and stir until smooth. Hot catsup: Combine prepared hot
mustard with catsup to desired hotness.

Any cut of pork may be used, but tenderness will vary according to cut.
Best to use boneless pork loin or tenderloin. Tougher cuts require longer
cooking time. Pork strips keep well frozen in whole piece after roasting.
Reheat if desired and slice before serving.

BARBECUED PORK II.
(This is a variation of the first recipe and is just as tasty.)

2-3   lbs lean pork roast cut into 2½"x2"x7" strips

Marinade

3 T	hoisin sauce
3 T	catsup
½ t	five spice powder
1 T	mirin
2 T	sugar
½ t	salt
1 t	ginger, minced
1 t	garlic, minced

1. Marinate meat at least 2 hours or overnight. If marinating overnight, cover meat and place in refrigerator.

2. Line a pan with foil and cover with ¼ inch of water. Place a rack over the pan of water. Arrange pork strips on rack and roast at 350° for approximately 1 hour and 10 minutes or until done.

3. Turn and baste meat with extra sauce every ½ hour.

4. Allow meat to cool slightly before slicing.

5. Slice ¼ inch thick and serve with hot mustard, catsup, and toasted sesame seeds.

BARBECUED SPARERIBS

1	side of pork spareribs (lean) 3 lbs.
1 t	salt
1 T	Chinese wine

Marinade

¼ C	hoisin sauce
¼ C	catsup
1 T	mirin
2 T	sugar
1 t	minced ginger root
1	clove garlic, minced

1. Mix together marinade.
2. Rub salt and wine on ribs.
3. Spread marinade on both sides of the spareribs.
4. Marinate about 2 hours.
5. Place ribs on rack of broiler pan with water in bottom of pan.
6. Roast for 1 hour and 15 minutes or until done at 375°. Turn and baste as needed.
7. Cut into bite size pieces or leave as whole ribs.

●

Spareribs are sometimes sold cut into 1½ inch strips for sweet and sour spareribs. Do not cut between the bones. Roast first, then cut into individual pieces so they will not dry out.

This recipe is also good as appetizers served warm.

SWEET AND SOUR SPARERIBS
(4 servings)

1 T   oil

2 lbs   spareribs cut into 1 ½ inch pieces

Sauce

¾ C   water
2 T   cornstarch
2 T   soy sauce
3 T   rice vinegar
⅔ C   sugar

Garnish

tomato, green pepper, pineapple chunks and toasted sesame seeds

1. Brown ribs in oil for 5 minutes and drain excess oil.
2. Mix together sauce and add to spareribs, stirring constantly until sauce thickens. Cover and simmer for ½ hour.
3. Garnish with tomato, green pepper, pineapple chunks and toasted sesame seeds.

●

Pork cubes may be used in this recipe. This dish keeps warm very well.
For sweet and sour fried pork: follow recipe for sweet and sour chicken.

BLACK BEAN SAUCE SPARERIBS
(4 servings)

1 T	oil
1 ½ lb	spareribs cut into 1 ½" pieces
1 T	salted black beans, rinsed
2	cloves garlic
1 t	ginger root
1 C	soup stock
2 t	dark soy sauce
1 T	mirin
¼ t.	salt
½ t	sugar
1 t	cornstarch dissolved in 1 t water
	chopped green onions

1. Brown spareribs in oil on high heat for 5 minutes. Drain excess fat.
2. Mash black beans, garlic and ginger. Add to spareribs and cook ½ minute.
3. Add soup stock, soy sauce, mirin, salt and sugar. Cover and simmer 15 to 20 minutes.
4. There should be small amount of liquid left. Add cornstarch mixture to thicken. Garnish with green onions.

•

Pork cubes may be used instead of spareribs.

For a variation:

Eliminate the 1 T oil, combine all other ingredients, mix together. Place in heatproof dish and steam the whole dish for 25 minutes. Garnish with green onions.

ALMOND BREADED PORK
(4-6 servings)

8-10   slices boneless pork loin (⅜ inch thick)

1 t   salt

½ C   all purpose flour
1   egg beaten
1½ C   panko (dehydrated bread crumbs)
¼ C   sliced almonds or walnuts

3 C   oil for deep frying (375°)

2 C   shredded cabbage

1. Salt pork slices.
2. Combine panko with sliced almonds.
3. Coat pork slices with flour, egg and press on panko mixture.
4. Fry in hot oil (375°) until golden brown. About 3-4 minutes.
5. Cut pork in bite-size pieces and arrange over cabbage.
6. Serve with hot mustard or other dips.

FRIED PORK ON SKEWERS
(18-20 skewers)

1 lb	boneless pork
1	large onion
2	medium green peppers
	salt and pepper

½ C	flour
2	eggs beaten
2 C	panko (dehydrated bread crumbs)

6"	bamboo skewers
	oil for deep frying (375°)

1. Cut the pork into 2"x1"x½" slices.
2. Cut onion and peppers into 2 inch squares.
3. Salt and pepper the pieces of pork.
4. Arrange ingredients on skewers.
5. Roll in flour, then egg and press on panko. Heat 2 inches of oil in a frying pan or wok and deep fry skewered items at 375° until golden brown, about 4 minutes.

STEAMED GROUND PORK

(4 servings)

¾ lb	lean ground pork
2	Chinese sausages, chopped
2 T	chopped water chestnuts
2	forest mushrooms (soaked, rinsed and chopped)
½ t	salt
2 t	soy sauce
1 T	cornstarch

1. Combine all ingredients thoroughly.
2. Spread mixture in an even layer over the bottom of a heat proof plate with a rim.
3. Steam for ½ hour. Serve hot.

•

Use other combinations of meats and vegetables.

Pork and Szechuan vegetables can be chopped or sliced. Use the same recipe omitting Chinese sausage, water chestnuts and mushrooms. Be sure to rinse off chili pepper before using Szechuan vegetable.

STEAMED FU YU SPARERIBS
(4 servings)

1½ lbs lean spareribs cut into 1½ inch pieces

3 T   fu yu (fermented white bean curd)
½ t   salt

1. Combine spareribs with fu yu and mix thoroughly, adding the salt.
2. Spread evenly in a heatproof bowl or dish with a rim.
3. Steam for ½ hour or until done.

●

This is a very easy and delicious recipe.
Substitute hoisin sauce or sweet bean sauce for the fu yu.
Use slices of pork instead of spareribs.
The sauce from these various dishes is delicious over hot steamed white rice.

PINEAPPLE BEEF KABOBS
(25 kabobs)

25   4" bamboo skewers
1 lb   sukiyaki beef strips (bacon thin slices of beef)
25   chunks green pepper or mushrooms
25   chunks pineapple

Sauce

¼ C   soy sauce
2 T   sugar
2 T   mirin
2   cloves garlic, crushed
1 t   ginger crushed

1. Marinate beef in sauce for ½ hour.
2. Roll strip of beef into a ball and place on skewer, alternating with green pepper, another beef strip, and top with a pineapple chunk.
3. Place kabobs on broiling pan and bake 10 minutes at 425°.

●

Delicious served with rice as a main course. Pour drippings from pan over kabobs.

Other vegetables may be used, such as chunks of tomato or onions.

Chunks of chicken breast cut into ½ inch thick pieces may be substituted for the beef. (No need to roll chicken.)

BROILED GINGER STEAK
(4 servings)

1½-2 lbs tender steak

Sauce

⅓ C   soy sauce
¼ C   mirin
2   cloves garlic, minced
2 t   chopped ginger

1. Marinate steaks for one hour in the sauce.
2. Broil steaks until done.
3. Slice into half inch thick slices to serve.
4. Bring remaining sauce to a boil, pour sauce over slices of steak.

GINGER BEEF
(4 servings)

1 lb	flank steak sliced thin against the grain
2 t	soy sauce
2 t	cornstarch
1 t	sugar
2 t	rice wine
2 T	oil
8	slices ginger root
½ C	soup stock
½ t	sugar
½ t	salt or to taste

cornstarch and water for thickening

1. Mix meat with soy sauce, cornstarch, sugar and wine. Set aside.
2. Heat wok and add the oil. Add ginger slices, fry about ½ minute on high heat.
3. Add beef, cook about 1 minute or until done. Push meat up the side of the wok.
4. Add soup stock, sugar and salt. Bring to a boil, thicken with cornstarch mixture.

●

Other cuts of beef may be used instead of flank steak.

OYSTER SAUCE STEAK
WITH MUSHROOMS
(4 servings)

3 T	oil
1 lb	flank steak
1 T	cornstarch
1 T	soy sauce
1 t	sugar
½ lb	fresh mushrooms
2 T	oyster sauce
½ C	water
1 T	cornstarch dissolved in 1 T water

1. Slice steak ¼ inch thick against the grain. Mix with cornstarch. soy sauce and sugar. Set aside.
2. Slice mushrooms ¼ inch thick.
3. Heat wok and add 1 T oil. Stir fry the mushrooms for 1 minute on high heat, remove and set aside.
4. Heat wok with the remaining 2 T oil and stir fry the beef until done.
5. Add oyster sauce and water, bring to a boil. Add salt to taste if desired.
6. Thicken with cornstarch and water. Add mushrooms, stir to combine ingredients.

•

Blanch one bunch of tender spinach, place on platter and serve with beef poured over spinach.

SESAME SEED STEAK
(4 servings)

1 lb   thinly sliced flank steak

Marinade

1 T	sesame seed oil
1 T	mirin
¼ C	soy sauce
1 T	sugar
1 t	minced garlic
¼ t	black pepper
2 t	minced fresh ginger root
1 T	toasted sesame seeds ground

¼ C   chopped green onions

Optional

Assorted vegetables thinly sliced, 1 medium onion, 1 green pepper, and ¼ lb. fresh mushrooms.

1. Combine meat with marinade and set aside until ready to use.

2. Add green onions just before cooking.

3. Meat may be placed on skewers and charcoal broiled or broiled in the oven, or just **pan broil** with small amounts of sesame seed oil added as needed.

To pan broil:

Use electric frying pan. Set temperature at 300°, turn temperature down as needed. Add sesame seed oil and cook beef and vegetables while eating. Serve with white rice.

BEEF TOMATO
(4 servings)

½ lb	beef sliced thin against the grain
2 t	soy sauce
2 t	cornstarch
1 t	sugar
2 T	oil
1	small onion, wedged
1	small green pepper, wedged
½ C	sliced fresh mushrooms
¼ C	catsup
1 T	sugar
½ t	salt
⅓ C	water
2	tomatoes, wedged

cornstarch and water for thickening

1. Combine beef slices with soy sauce, cornstarch and sugar. Set aside.
2. Heat wok and add the oil. Stir fry the beef slices until done, push up to the sides of the wok.
3. Add onions, peppers and mushrooms, stir fry a few seconds.
4. Add catsup, sugar, salt, and water. Bring to a boil and toss in tomato wedges.
5. Thicken with cornstarch and water mixture. Stir gently to combine.

•

Do not serve this dish with a sweet and sour course in the same meal.

BEEF MEATBALLS
(20 meatballs)

Meat mixture

1 ½ lbs ground beef
1   clove garlic, minced
1 t   minced ginger root
1 T   soy sauce
1 ½ T cornstarch
⅓ C   finely chopped onions
⅓ C   finely chopped fresh mushrooms
½ t   salt

2 T   oil

1 lb   leafy green vegetable, sliced
½ t   salt

1 T   rice wine
2 t   soy sauce
1 C   soup stock
½ t   salt or to taste

        cornstarch and water for thickening

1. Thoroughly combine the meat mixture and shape into 20 meatballs.
2. Heat wok, add 1 T oil and stir fry leafy greens on high heat just until limp, adding ½ t salt. Remove to a platter and set aside.
3. Heat a skillet or wok with 1 T oil and slowly fry meatballs on medium high heat until all sides are light brown. Drain off excess fat.
4. Turn heat to high, add wine, soy sauce, soup stock and salt. Cover bring to a boil, turn temperature down and simmer for 10 minutes.
5. Return temperature to high and thicken with cornstarch mixture to form a medium thick gravy. Serve over the bed of leafy greens.

●

Pork may be used instead of beef or use a combination of both.

The meat mixture is delicious made into regular hamburgers.

Any vegetable may be used such as celery, cabbage, broccoli, or even frozen green peas. Make sure vegetables are cooked until tender by adding a little water to the pan while stir frying the vegetables.

CURRY BEEF
(4-6 servings)

1½ lb   boneless beef cut into 1½ inch cubes (3 cups)
2 T   flour
1 T   soy sauce
1 T   rice wine

2 T   oil
2   cloves garlic, minced
1   large onion cut into wedges
1½ T   curry powder

1 T   catsup
1½ t   salt
1 t   sugar
1 C   water or soup stock

2   large potatoes (peeled and cut into wedges)
3   carrots (peeled and sliced ½ inch thick)

1. Coat beef cubes with flour, soy sauce and wine.

2. Heat the oil in a large sauce pan and slowly brown the beef on medium high heat for about 10 minutes.

3. Add the garlic, onions and curry powder. Stir fry about ½ minute. Add catsup, salt, sugar and soup stock. Cover, bring to a boil and simmer 40 minutes.

4. Add potatoes and carrots, stir to mix. Cover and simmer slowly for 20 minutes more.

Serve with hot steamed rice.

•

Make ahead and reheat ½ hour on low heat.

SPICY BEEF WITH GREEN PEPPER
(4 servings)

3 T	oil
½ lb	beef steak
2 t	soy sauce
1 t	sugar
2 t	cornstarch
1	clove garlic, minced
1 t	minced ginger root
1½ t	hot bean paste
1	green pepper cut into shreds
1 t	rice wine
½ t	sugar
½ t	salt
1 t	sesame seed oil
1½ T	hoisin sauce (optional)
¼ C	shredded green onions

1. Slice beef thin against the grain. Then cut into shreds to resemble bean sprouts.
2. Coat beef with soy sauce, sugar and cornstarch.
3. Heat wok, add 2 T oil and stir fry beef until done. Remove from wok and set aside.
4. Add 1 T oil to wok, fry garlic, ginger and hot bean paste for a few seconds.
5. Add shredded green pepper and stir to combine ingredients.
6. Add rice wine, sugar, salt and sesame seed oil. Stir in hoisin sauce if desired.
7. Return beef to wok, mix in green onions and cook ½ minute to thoroughly combine ingredients.

•

Serve this dish with lettuce cups, use the small inside leaves of a head of lettuce as a cup. Scoop some beef into the cups and eat like a sandwich.

Substitute shredded carrots for the green pepper.

Nowhere is the importance of bringing out the natural flavor of food more evident than in the preparation of fish and shellfish. The key to delicious seafood is freshness. Fresh fish will exhibit firm flesh, round clear eyes, bright red gills, and a mild fresh odor.

Seafood

POACHED WHOLE FISH
(4-6 servings)

1	2½-3 sea bass, cleaned (retain head and tail)
1	green onion
2	slices ginger root
¼ t	white pepper
¼ C	soy sauce
1 T	sesame seed oil
¼ C	slivered, pickled ginger and vegetables
2	green onions, slivered in 2-inch lengths
¼ C	oil (heated until hot)

1. In a large pot, bring to a boil enough water to cover the fish. Add ginger, green onion and the fish. Cover pot, turn temperature to the lowest setting and poach 25 minutes or until done.

2. Remove fish carefully with a large metal strainer and spatula. Place on a large platter.

3. Sprinkle white pepper over fish. Pour soy sauce and sesame seed oil on top of fish. Arrange pickles and green onions on top of fish.

4. Heat the ¼ cup oil until hot and pour over fish and green onions. The ingredients should sizzle.

Use about 2 T of fresh slivered ginger root instead of pickled ginger and vegetables, if desired.

●

Pickled ginger and vegetables are sold in cans. Once opened, keep in a jar sealed tightly in the refrigerator. Keeps for several weeks.

Any firm fish can be cooked this way. Try this recipe with salmon steaks or fillets. Be sure to adjust poaching time so fish does not overcook.

STEAMED ROCK COD
(4 servings)

1	2½-3 lb rock cod, cleaned (retain head and tail)

¼ t	white pepper
1 T	sesame seed oil
¼ C	slivered green onions
1 T	slivered ginger root
⅓ C	soy sauce
¼ C	oil (heated until hot)

1. Place clean fish on a heatproof plate with a rim. If fish is too long, cut in half and place side by side.

2. Bring 4 cups of water to a boil in the wok or steamer. Place plate of fish on a rack over the boiling water. Cover wok and steam on high heat for 25 minutes or until done. Check water level during steaming. Make sure there is good steam circulation during steaming time.

3. Remove plate of fish from steamer. Drain off liquid from the platter or carefully remove fish to another plate.

4. Sprinkle white pepper over fish. Pour sesame seed oil on top of fish.

5. Add green onions and ginger root. Pour soy sauce over the ingredients.

6. Heat ¼ cup oil until hot. Pour over all ingredients to sizzle green onions and fish.

●

This recipe is delicious with any kind of fish. Fish steaks or fillets are also good. Adjust steaming time for thickness of fish. Allow 10 minutes of steaming time for every one inch of thickness.

STEAMED FISH WITH PORK
(4 servings)

2 lbs	fresh fish fillet (cleaned and dried)
1 t	salt
1 C	pork
4	medium forest mushrooms (soaked and rinsed)
25	tiger lily buds (soaked and rinsed. Remove any hard knobs)
1 T	rice wine
1 T	soy sauce
1 t	cornstarch
2	green onions, cut in 1 inch slivers
¼ C	oil (heat until hot)

1. Place fish on heatproof platter with a rim.
2. Coat fish with salt.
3. Slice pork and mushrooms in thin slivers. Cut tiger lily buds in half. Place in a bowl and mix with wine, soy sauce and cornstarch.
4. Place mixture over fish.
5. Steam for 25 minutes.
6. Remove and top with green onions.
7. Heat oil until hot and pour over green onions and meat.

●

Fish can be steamed this way without meat mixture. Steam fish until done. Pour off liquid and season with ¼ C soy sauce poured over fish. Sprinkle ginger and green onion slivers over fish and pour on hot oil.

STEAMED FISH WITH SOY BEAN PASTE
(4 servings)

1 ½ lbs fish steaks or fillets

¼ C	red soy bean paste (Japanese red miso)
1 T	slivered ginger root
1 T	sesame seed oil
2	green onions, chopped
2 T	oil (heated until hot)

1. Clean fish and dry with paper towels. Place in a heatproof plate with a rim.
2. Spread a thin layer of miso over the top of the pieces of fish.
3. Sprinkle with ginger and sesame seed oil.
4. Place on a steamer and steam for 15 to 20 minutes.
5. Toss green onions over fish and sizzle with hot oil.

●

This recipe is good to use with any kind of fish steaks or fillets. Omit the hot oil to reduce calories.

STEAMED FISH WITH GINGER

1 ½ lb	white fish fillets
⅛ t	white pepper
2 T	sesame seed oil
¼ C	soy sauce
1 T	slivered fresh ginger root
¼ C	slivered green onions
¼ C	hot oil

1. Clean and thoroughly dry fish with paper towel.
2. Place fish in a heat proof dish and place in a steamer.
3. Steam fish about 10 minutes for each inch of thickness.
4. Remove fish from steamer, pour out excess liquid.
5. Sprinkle with pepper, sesame seed oil, soy sauce, ginger root and green onion.
6. Pour hot oil over fish to sizzle ingredients.

SWEET AND SOUR FISH
(4-6 servings)

1	2-3 lb fish (rock cod, sea bass or fillets)
1 T	wine
1 t	salt
½ C	all purpose flour
½ C	cornstarch
2	eggs, beaten
5 C	oil for deep frying
2 T	oil
1	clove garlic, minced
1 T	slivered ginger root
4	medium forest mushrooms (soaked, rinsed and sliced)
1	carrot, peeled and slivered
½ C	slivered green peppers
2	green onions, slivered

Sauce Ingredients

¼ C	rice vinegar
¼ C	sugar
3 T	catsup
½ t	chili pepper
1 T	rice wine
¼ t	salt
1 t	sesame seed oil
½ C	water
5 t	cornstarch

1. Clean and dry fish. Cut 3 slashes on both sides of the fish, 1 inch apart. Rub with wine and salt.

2. Combine flour and cornstarch. Coat fish with mixture, dip in eggs, then again in flour mixture.

3. Fry in 375° oil for 15 minutes, turning once. Remove and place on a platter.

4. Heat 2 T oil in wok, fry garlic, ginger, mushrooms, carrots, and green peppers for ½ minute.

5. Add all sauce ingredients, stir and bring to a boil, adding green onions.

6. Serve sauce over fish.

●

Fillet of red snapper or any firm white fish fillet may be used.

FRIED OYSTERS
(Method I)
(4 servings)

½ lb   fresh shelled oysters, rinsed and drained

      salt

½ C   all purpose flour
2   eggs, beaten
1 C   panko (dehydrated bread crumbs)

3 C   oil for deep frying (375°)

1. Dry oysters thoroughly. Lightly salt oysters.

2. Coat with flour, dip in egg and press on panko.

3. Deep fry 2 to 3 minutes or until golden brown. May also be pan fried.

FRIED OYSTERS
(Method II)

½ lb   fresh shelled oysters, rinsed and drained
      boiling water
      salt

Batter

½ C   all purpose flour
¼ C   cornstarch
1 t   baking powder
½ t   baking soda
⅔ C   cold water

3 C   oil for deep frying (375°)

1. Put oysters in boiling water and cook for about ½ minute. Drain thoroughly and pat dry with paper towels.

2. If oysters are large, cut into smaller pieces about the size of a thumb.

3. Lighlty salt oysters.

4. Mix batter. Dip into batter and deep fry until golden brown.

●

Serve with hot mustard or hot catsup.

Hot mustard: 1 T powder to 1 T water.

Hot catsup: Combine prepared hot mustard with catsup to desired hotness.

DEEP FRIED SKEWERED SEAFOOD
(4-6 servings)

12	8 inch bamboo skewers
¾ lb	clams (12 clams)
½ lb	squid
½ lb	prawns
¼ lb	scallops
½ lb	cod or firm fish fillet
3	green onions cut into 1 ½ inch pieces
1 t	salt

Dip

½ C	all purpose flour	2 T	soy sauce
2	eggs, beaten	1 T	sugar
2½ C	panko (dehydrated bread crumbs)	1 t	sesame seed oil
		1	clove garlic, minced
4 C	oil for deep frying (375°)	1 t	minced ginger root
		½ t	hot soy bean paste or
2 C	shredded lettuce		chili paste with garlic

1. Cook clams in boiling water for 3 minutes. Remove from shells and drain. Set aside.

2. Cut off tentacles of the squid, reserve for another use. Open the cavity flat, discard contents and pull off outer speckled membrane. Rinse and dry with paper towels. Cut squid into 2 inch pieces. Set aside.

3. Shell prawns and devein. Rinse, dry with paper towels and set aside.

4. Have scallops and fish clean and dry. Cut into 1x1x1 ½ inch pieces. Set aside.

5. Arrange ingredients on skewers. Try to skewer each piece at least twice; bringing skewer in, then out.

6. Lightly salt each skewer of seafood.

7. Coat each skewer of seafood with flour, dusting off the excess. Dip in egg and press on panko.

8. Deep fry in 375° oil for approximately 4 minutes or until golden brown.

9. Serve skewers on top of a plate of shredded lettuce.

10. Have dip follow the skewers. Hot mustard or hot catsup may also be used as dips.

Oysters breaded this way without being skewered are delicious deep fried or pan fried.

Hot mustard: 1 T dry mustard powder dissolved in 1 T water. Stir until smooth.

Hot catsup: Combine prepared hot mustard with catsup to desired hotness.

5 slices of white bread will yield 3 cups of bread crumbs. Process to course crumbs in a blender.

GARLIC SAUCE SHRIMP WITH PEPPERS

1 lb	prawns (shelled and deveined)
2 T	oil
1 C	diced green or red peppers
1 T	fermented black beans, rinsed and drained
2	large cloves garlic, minced
2	sliced fresh ginger root
2 T	rice wine
2 t	soy sauce
¼ t	salt
¼ c	soup stock
1 t	chili paste with garlic (optional)
	cornstarch and water for thickening
	green onions for garnish cut in one inch pieces

1. Cut prawns in half lengthwise, at the top end only. (Butterfly)

2. Mash the black beans with garlic and ginger. Set aside.

3. Heat oil in wok and stir fry the prawns for about 1 minute.

4. Add peppers and black bean mixture and cook ½ minute.

5. Add rice wine, soy sauce, salt, soup stock and chili paste. Bring to a boil, thicken with cornstarch and water mixture.

6. Garnish with green onions.

SHRIMP STUFFED CRAB CLAWS
(4 servings)

8-10   cooked king crab claws with upper half of shell removed.
1 lb   shrimp shelled, deveined, rinsed and patted dry
¼ C   bamboo shoots
1 t   wine
1 T   cornstarch
1   egg white
1 t   salt

Breading

½ C   flour
2   eggs beaten
2 C   panko (dehydrated bread crumbs)

     oil for deep frying (375°)

1. Remove some of crab meat and set aside, reserving claws.
2. Chop shrimp and bamboo shoots until smooth.
3. Mix in wine, cornstarch, egg white, salt and crab meat.
4. Stuff shrimp mixture on top of crab claws, reshaping to form original claw. Allow to chill ½ hour for easier handling.
5. Coat claws with flour, dip in egg and gently press on panko. May dip in egg and panko again for a thicker breading if desired.
6. Deep fry in oil (375°) for approximately 5 minutes or until golden brown.
7. Serve plain or dip in sweet and sour sauce.

●

Keeps warm in oven. May be made ahead without breading and freeze. Bread on day of serving.

Fantastic as an appetizer.

Pammie's favorite.

CRAB WITH BLACK BEAN SAUCE
(4 servings)

1	large cooked crab (2½ lbs.)
1 T	oil
½ lb	ground pork
1½ T	fermented black beans, rinsed and drained
2	cloves garlic, crushed
2	slices ginger root
1 t	sugar
2 T	oyster sauce
¼ t	salt
1 C	water
1	egg
2	green onions, chopped
	cornstarch and water for thickening

1. Remove outer shell of crab and discard. Rinse and clean crab. Cut crab in half. Holding each leg by the cavity, break off a section of the center cavity with each leg. Crack legs, rinse off bits of shell, drain and set aside.

2. Mash black beans with garlic, ginger and sugar. Set aside.

3. Heat wok and add oil. Stir fry pork on high heat until done (about 2 minutes). If there is excess fat from the pork, drain off.

4. Add black bean mixture and mix together with pork.

5. Add oyster sauce, salt and water. Stir to combine. Carefully place crab on top, cover wok, bring to a boil and cook 3 to 4 minutes to heat crab through.

6. Carefully remove crab pieces and place on a platter.

7. Add egg to mixture in the wok and stir. Toss in green onions and thicken with cornstarch and water mixture.

8. Pour entire mixture (called lobster sauce) over the crab.

●

Break off the pointed tips of the crab legs to help remove the crab meat from the shells.

Uncooked lobster tails may be substituted for the crab. Devein tails and cut into individual sections, shells intact. Follow recipe and add lobster after cooking the pork. Do **not** remove lobster from the wok during cooking.

CLAMS WITH BLACK BEAN SAUCE
(4 servings)

1 ½ lbs clams in shells (24 clams)

1 ½ T	black beans
1	large clove garlic
2	thin slices of ginger root
2 T	oil
2 t	soy sauce
1 T	mirin
1 T	rice wine
1 t	chili paste w/ soy bean
½ t	salt
½ C	water
1	green onion, chopped
	cornstarch for thickening

1. Soak clams in cold water with an iron knife for 4 hours to remove sand. Remove clams, rinse and drain.
2. Rinse black beans, drain. Mash beans with garlic and ginger to form a paste.
3. Heat oil in wok until hot, add clams and stir fry a few seconds.
4. Add black bean mixture to the bottom of wok and stir fry ½ minute.
5. Add soy sauce, mirin, rice wine, chili paste, salt and water. Cover, bring to a full boil and steam 3 minutes.
6. Add green onions and thicken with cornstarch and water to desired consistency.

•

Clams can also be soaked overnight in cold water with some corn meal to remove sand. Use scallops or fish as a substitute for clams. If scallops are small, leave whole. Slice fish into 1"x2"x½" slices.

STIR FRIED GEODUCK WITH VEGETABLES
(4-6 servings)

1	medium geoduck clam
1 T	rice wine
½ t	salt
¼ t	white pepper
1 t	sesame seed oil
2 t	cornstarch
3 T	oil
2	cloves garlic, minced
1 T	slivered ginger root
½ lb	pea pods (stringed, rinsed and drained)
1	small onion cut in wedges
¼ C	sliced water chestnuts
¼ C	sliced bamboo shoots
½ t	salt
2 T	soup stock or water
2 t	soy sauce
1 T	rice wine
2	green onions cut into 1 inch pieces

1. Place geoduck in the sink and run hot water on the neck of the clam until the skin separates from the neck. Run a knife around the inside of the shell to open the clam. Discard stomach and pull off neck. Cut off the very tip of the neck and slice open lengthwise. Rinse carefully to remove sand and skin.

2. Slice into thin ⅛ inch slices. Combine with rice wine, salt, pepper, sesame seed oil and cornstarch.

3. Heat wok and add 1 T oil. Add some of the garlic and allow to fry for a few seconds. Add vegetables and salt. Stir fry for about 1 minute, adding soup stock if necessary. Remove to a platter.

4. Clean wok. Heat wok and add 2 T oil. Fry garlic and ginger for a few seconds.

5. Add clam slices and stir fry for about ½ minute. Add soy sauce and wine.

6. Toss in green onions. Salt to taste and serve over vegetables. Do not overcook clam slices or they will be tough.

●

Substitute clam slices with ½ lb. scallops sliced ¼ inch thick.

DEEP FRIED PRAWNS
(4 servings)

1 lb   prawns (24 prawns)
½ t   salt

Batter

½ C   all purpose flour
¼ C   cornstarch
1 t   baking powder
½ t   baking soda
⅔ C   cold water

3 C   oil for deep frying (375°)

1   lemon cut into wedges
     Chinese hot mustard and catsup

1. Shell prawns, retaining the tail. Open top of prawn just enough to remove the vein. Rinse and **dry prawns with paper towels.**
2. Salt prawns.
3. Mix together the batter.
4. Heat 3 cups of oil in the wok to 375°.
5. Dip prawns into batter and deep fry prawns for 2 to 3 minutes or until golden brown.
6. Serve with lemon wedges, hot mustard and hot catsup.

•

Hot mustard is purchased as a powder. To prepare, combine 1 T mustard to 1 T water and stir until smooth.

Hot catsup: Combine prepared hot mustard with catsup to desired hotness.

The above batter is excellent for fish or other shellfish. Cut fish into 3 inch pieces. Be sure to towel dry fish or other shellfish or batter will not adhere.

Sweet & Sour Prawns: Serve with sweet and sour sauce garnished with tomato, green pepper and pineapple chunks.

PRAWNS WITH LOBSTER SAUCE
(4 servings)

1 lb	prawns
3 T	oil
½ lb	ground pork
1 ½ T	fermented black beans, rinsed and drained
1	clove garlic, crushed
1	slice ginger root
1 t	sugar
2 T	oyster sauce
¼ t	salt
⅔ C	water
1	egg
1	green onion, chopped
	cornstarch and water for thickening

1. Shell prawns retaining tails. Devein and rinse.
2. Slice prawns in half lengthwise, at the top end only (butterfly).
3. Mash black beans with garlic, ginger and sugar. Set aside.
4. Heat wok. Add 2 T oil and stir fry prawns until they turn white and pink. Remove and set aside.
5. Add 1 T oil to wok and stir fry the pork about 2 minutes or until the pink color is gone.
6. Add black bean mixture, stir to combine.
7. Add oyster sauce, salt and water. Bring to a boil, cover wok and cook 1 minute.
8. Add prawns, cook about ½ minute.
9. Stir in egg, add green onions and thicken with cornstarch and water mixture.

●

The above recipe has no lobster but is called lobster sauce because traditionally lobster was cooked in combination with the pork and black beans.

Prawns may be substituted with scallops sliced ¼ inch thick or lobster meat.

PRAWNS WITH BLACK BEAN SAUCE
(4 servings)

1 lb	prawns
2 T	oil
1 T	fermented black beans, rinsed and drained
1	large clove garlic, crushed
2	slices ginger root
1 T	mirin or sherry
1 T	soy sauce
¼ t	salt
¼ C	water
	cornstarch and water for thickening
2	green onions cut in one inch pieces

1. Shell prawns retaining the tail. Devein and rinse.
2. Slice prawns in half lengthwise, at the top end only. (Butterfly)
3. Mash the black beans with garlic and ginger. Set aside.
4. Heat wok and add 2 T oil. Stir fry the prawns for about 1 minute.
5. Add black bean mixture and cook ½ minute.
6. Add mirin, soy sauce, salt and water. Bring to a boil, cooking prawns.
7. Thicken with cornstarch and water mixture. Toss in green onions.

●

Slices of fish or scallops can be substituted for the prawns. Also thin slices of chicken breast can be used instead of prawns.

SHRIMP WITH GREEN PEAS
(4 servings)

½ lb	prawns
½ t	salt
½	egg white
2 t	cornstarch
2 T	oil
2 t	minced ginger root
1 C	frozen green peas (defrosted)
¼ t	salt
1 T	rice wine
	chopped green onions

1. Shell prawns, cut in half lengthwise, remove vein, rinse and pat dry.
2. Coat prawns with salt, **egg** white and cornstarch.
3. Heat wok, add oil. Add prawns, cook about ½ minute.
4. Add ginger root, peas, salt and wine. Cook 1 minute.
5. Toss in green onions.

●

This recipe is delicious as a filling for Mandarin pancakes.

TOMATO SAUCE PRAWNS
(2 servings)

½ lb	prawns
2 T	oil
1	small onion, wedged
1	green pepper, wedged
¼ C	catsup
1 T	sugar
½ t	salt
¼ C	water
2	tomatoes, wedged
	cornstarch and water for thickening

1. Shell prawns, retaining the tail. Devein and rinse.
2. Slice prawns in half lengthwise, at the top end only (butterfly).
3. Heat wok and add oil. Add prawns, onions and green peppers. Stir fry until prawns turn white, about 1 minute.
4. Add catsup, sugar, salt and water. Bring to a boil, cooking prawns.
5. Add tomatoes, and thicken with cornstarch to desired thickness.

●

Celery and green onions can be added to the recipe.
Try this recipe over pan fried noodles.

SPICY PRAWNS
(4 servings)

¾ lb	prawns
2 T	oil
1	clove garlic, minced
1 t	minced ginger root
2 t	hot bean paste
¼ C	catsup
3 T	rice wine
½ t	salt
1 T	sugar
¼ C	chopped onions

1. Remove vein from the tops of the prawns carefully. Rinse and pat dry (do not shell the prawns).
2. Heat wok and add oil. Add prawns, garlic and ginger. Stir fry 1 minute.
3. Add hot bean paste, catsup, wine, salt and sugar. Bring to a boil, cooking prawns (1 minute).
4. Toss in green onions.

●

The shell of the prawn is in sections. If the vein breaks, go to the next section and try to remove the vein. If this is too difficult, cook the prawns shelled. The shell of the prawn retains the moisture when cooked.

JELLY FISH CUCUMBER SALAD
(4-6 servings)

2.4 oz. package of salted shredded jelly fish

1	medium cucumber (1 ½ C slivered)
2	stalks celery (1 C slivered)

½ C	slivered ham
½ C	slivered cooked chicken breast

Dressing

3 T	rice vinegar
2 T	sugar
1 T	soy sauce
1 T	sesame seed oil

1. Rinse salt off jelly fish. Soak jelly fish in cold water to cover for one hour and drain. Cover with cold water and allow to soak for 2 more hours. Drain jelly fish and place in a strainer. Pour a small amount of hot water over jelly fish and immediately cool with cold water. Squeeze dry, cut in 3" lengths and set aside. (If water is too hot, jelly fish will be too curly.)
2. Cut cucumber in half and remove seeds. Cut cucumber halves in 2 inch lengths. Slice in thin pieces lengthwise, then sliver to resemble beansprouts.
3. Cut celery in the same manner to resemble beansprouts.
4. Arrange all ingredients attractively in a bowl with the jelly fish on top.
5. Combine dressing and pour over salad. Toss to combine.

●

If jelly fish is not available, use bean threads (saifun) 1.4 oz. Soak saifun in hot water for half an hour. Drain and cut into 3 inch lengths. Combine with other ingredients.

Other vegetables such as daikon, and meats such as cooked shrimp, may be used as substitutes.

FOIL WRAPPED SALMON
(4 servings)

4   6 oz. slices of salmon fillet

Marinade

4 T   vegetable oil
1 t   salt
2 t   sugar
1 T   soy sauce
3   egg yolks
2 T   sesame seeds

1   medium onion, diced
1   small carrot, diced and parboiled
1   small green pepper, diced
4   medium forest mushrooms (soaked, rinsed and diced)

4   pieces of foil to wrap ingredients

1. Combine marinade ingredients. Soak salmon in marinade for ½ hour.
2. Place one piece of salmon on foil and arrange other ingredients on top.
3. Pour some of marinade over each package, wrap air tight and bake in a 425° oven for 20 to 25 minutes.

●

White fish can be substituted for the salmon. Omit egg yolk from marinade. Use slices of lemon placed on top of fish with other ingredients.

SEAFOOD CASSEROLE
(4 servings)

1 ½ lbs white fish fillet, cut in 2 inch chunks
½ lb   shrimp (shelled, deveined and cut in half lengthwise)
¼ lb   squid, cleaned and cut in 2 inch pieces
10   leaves Chinese cabbage sliced in 2 inch pieces
1   bunch spinach, washed and stems removed
1 C   bamboo shoots, sliced
4   large forest mushrooms (soaked, rinsed and sliced ½ inch thick)

Sauce

4 C   soup stock
2 T   soy sauce
1 t   salt
¼ C   rice wine
1 T   sugar

1. Arrange all ingredients on a large platter.
2. In a large heatproof casserole, combine sauce ingredients and bring to a slow simmer.
3. Place ingredients in a casserole and cook just until done. Remove a selection of food onto a small dish and also some broth. Serve with a selection of sauces or spices.

Vinegar and soy sauce or a squeeze of lemon with a dash of pepper is good as a dip.

●

This makes a very nice one dish winter meal. A variety of fish or vegetables may be used as the seasons change.

162

SPICY CUCUMBER CHICKEN SALAD

2 oz.	bean threads, soaked
1	cucumber, shredded
2 C	shredded lettuce
1	cooked chicken breast shredded
or	
1 C	cooked tiny shrimp
¼ C	chopped green onions

Dressing

2 T	sesame seed paste or chunky peanut butter
1 T	soy sauce
1 t	sugar
1 t	sesame seed oil
1 t	hot pepper oil
1 t	rice vinegar
1 T	chopped green onions
2	cloves garlic, minced
2 t	fresh minced ginger root
¼ C	soup stock

1. Bring a pot of water to a boil and cook bean threads for 2 minutes.
2. Rinse bean threads in cold water and drain thoroughly. Place in a large platter.
3. Arrange all other ingredients on top.
4. Pour on dressing just before serving.

These ingredients are essential to a variety of meatless and almost meatless courses. In addition, they are very economical to buy and high in nutritional content. A multitude of vegetables are available through your local markets.

Fresh bean curd is sold in 12 to 16 ounce creamy white blocks. Bean curd, more commonly known as tofu, is rich in protein, vitamins and minerals, but low in calories, saturated fats, and free of cholesterol.

Vegetable, Eggs & Tofu

CHICKEN MAIFUN SALAD
(4-6 servings)

3 C	oil for deep frying
2½ oz.	maifun (rice sticks)
3	forest mushrooms
1 C	cooked, shredded chicken breast
2 C	shredded lettuce
¼ C	chopped green onions
e T	toasted sesame seeds
½ C	toasted slivered almonds

Dressing

¼ C	rice vinegar
¼ C	vegetable oil
1 t	sesame seed oil
2 T	sugar
¼ t	black pepper
½ t	salt

1. Heat 3 cups of oil in the wok to 400°. Put in one rice stick. If it puffs up immediately, put in a small handful. Turn rice sticks over to allow the sticks on top to puff. Remove immediately. Set aside.

2. Soak mushrooms until soft, rinse and boil in some water for 10 minutes. Remove and allow to cool. Squeeze dry and slice into thin strips.

3. Have all other ingredients cut and ready.

4. Combine all ingredients and toss with dressing just before serving.

●

An easy way to cook the chicken breast is to poach in water until done, about half an hour. Bring water to a boil first, add chicken breast, cover pot and simmer for ½ hour.

Have all ingredients separate and combine just before serving. Maifun can be puffed ahead and kept in a plastic bag until ready to use.

To toast almonds: Place in 350° oven and bake 10 minutes.

CHICKEN WITH VEGETABLES AND PEPPERS
(4 servings)

3 T	oil
1	boneless chicken breast, sliced ¼ inch thick against the grain
1	clove garlic, minced
1 t	oil
2 t	cornstarch
1 t	rice wine
¼ t	white pepper
½ t	sugar
1	small green pepper cut in wedges
1	small red pepper cut in wedges
½	small onion cut in wedges
10	pea pods (remove strings)
¼ C	sliced water chestnuts
½ C	baby corn
1 T	minced fresh hot chili pepper
½ t	salt or to taste
1 T	rice wine
¼ C	soup stock

1. Combine chicken with garlic, oil, cornstarch, wine, pepper and sugar. Set aside.
2. Prepare other ingredients.
3. Heat wok and add oil. Stir fry chicken on medium high heat until it turns white. Remove and set aside.
4. Turn heat to high, add all other ingredients, cover and cook 1 minute. Remove cover, add chicken and cook until most of the liquid is cooked away.

•

Other vegetables may be added or substituted. Try using cloud ears or forest mushrooms.

Substitute thin sliced carrots for the red pepper.

DICED CHICKEN WITH VEGETABLES
AND ALMONDS
(4 servings)

2 T	oil
1	chicken breast, boned and diced
6	large prawns (shelled, deveined, rinsed and diced)
1	small onion, diced
1	celery stalk, diced
½ C	diced bamboo shoots
¼ C	diced water chestnuts
½ C	button mushrooms
½ C	frozen green peas, defrosted
1 T	mirin
1 t	salt
½ C	water or soup stock
	cornstarch and water for thickening
½ C	toasted whole almonds

1. All meats and vegetables should be diced in ½ inch cubes.
2. Heat wok, add 2 T oil and stir fry the chicken for 2 minutes on high heat.
3. Add prawns and stir fry for ½ minute.
4. Add all ingredients except cornstarch and almonds. Cover wok, bring to a boil and cook 1 minute.
5. Thicken with cornstarch mixture. Remove to a serving dish and garnish with toasted almonds on top.

●

Pork may be substituted for the chicken. Use other vegetables such as diced green beans, asparagus, broccoli stems, carrots or peppers.

Cashew nuts may be used instead of almonds. Toast almonds in the oven for 10-15 minutes at 350°.

PEA PODS WITH BEEF
(4 servings)

1 lb	fresh pea pods
¼ lb	beef, sliced thin against the grain
1 t	soy sauce
½ t	sugar
1 t	cornstarch
3 T	oil
1	clove garlic, minced
1 T	oyster sauce
¼ t	salt or to taste
¼ C	soup stock
	cornstarch and water for thickening if needed

1. Break tips of pea pods and remove strings. Rinse and drain.
2. Combine beef with soy sauce, sugar and cornstarch. Set aside.
3. Heat wok, add 1½ T oil, garlic and the beef. Stir fry the beef until done, remove and set aside.
4. Add 1½ T oil to wok. Stir fry pea pods for ½ minute. Add oyster sauce, salt and soup stock. Bring to a boil, cooking pea pods just until tender (½ minute).
5. Add beef to pea pods. Thicken with cornstarch and water mixture to form a medium thick sauce if desired.

●

Chinese long beans: 1 lb. Snap off ends of beans and cut beans into 2 inch lengths. Follow above recipe.

Bitter melon (fu gwa): 1 lb. Cut bitter melon in half lengthwise and remove seeds. Rinse melon halves and drain. Slice melon into ¼ inch thick pieces. Follow above recipe.

Most any vegetable can be used in the above recipe. Prepare vegetable for cooking and adjust cooking time and soup stock needed according to how long the vegetable needs to be cooked to be crisp tender.

Substitute other meats for beef to obtain a variation of this dish.

BROCCOLI WITH BEEF
(4 servings)

2 T   oil

½ lb   flank steak, sliced thin against the grain
2 t   cornstarch
2 t   soy sauce
½ t   sugar

1 ½ lb   broccoli
½ t   salt
½ C   soup stock

        cornstarch for thickening

1. Combine beef with cornstarch, soy sauce and sugar. Set aside.
2. Cut broccoli flowerets into 2 inch lengths, separating into small clusters. Peel stem and cut in ½ inch thick diagonal slices.
3. Heat wok, add oil and stir fry beef slices on high heat until done. Remove and set aside.
4. Add broccoli to wok. Add salt and soup stock. Cover wok, bring to a boil and cook 2-3 minutes.
5. Return beef to wok and thicken with cornstarch mixture. Stir to combine all ingredients.

●

This recipe is good for dense vegetables such as cauliflower, green beens and asparagus.

Cauliflower: Separate into flowerets. Slice into ½ inch thick slices.

Green Beans: String the beans and cut into 2 inch lengths. If the beans are too thick, cut into ½ inch thick diagonal slices.

Asparagus: Snap off ends of asparagus and slice into ½ inch thick diagonal slices.

CHINESE GREENS WITH BEEF
(2 servings)

½ lb   beef
2 t   cornstarch
2 t   soy sauce
1 t   sugar

1 ½ lb   Chinese greens (bok choy)

1 T   oil

½ C   soup stock
½ t   salt

2 t   cornstarch dissolved in 1 T water

1. Slice beef ¼" thick against the grain.
2. Marinate beef in cornstarch, soy sauce and sugar.
3. Cut bok choy in ½" diagonal slices.
4. Heat 2 T oil in wok and stir fry beef on high heat until done; remove from wok and set aside.
5. Add 1 T oil and stir fry bok choy on high heat for ½ minute. Add soup stock, salt, cover, bring to boil and steam 1 minute.
6. Return beef to wok and mix, add enough cornstarch mixture to thicken. Serve with white rice.

•

Other vegetables may be substituted. Adjust steaming time and soup stock.

Dense vegetables such as broccoli require longer cooking, more soup stock required.

Use other meats such as pork or chicken; do not remove from wok. Allow other meats to cook with the vegetable.

BITTER MELON WITH BEEF
(4 servings)

2	large bitter melons or approximately 1 lb.

¼ lb	beef, sliced thin against the grain
1 t	rice wine
2 t	soy sauce
1 t	sugar
2 t	cornstarch

1½ T	salted black beans, rinsed and drained
1	clove garlic, crushed
1	slice ginger root

3 T	oil

1 t	sugar or 1 T mirin
¼ t	salt
½ C	soup stock

cornstarch and water for thickening

1. Split melons in half lengthwise and remove seeds. Rinse and dry melon halves. Slice into ¼ inch thick slices. Set aside.
2. Combine beef slices with wine, soy sauce, sugar and cornstarch. Set aside.
3. Mash black beans, garlic and ginger to form a paste. Set aside.
4. Heat wok, add 1½ T oil and stir fry beef until done, remove and set aside.
5. Add remaining 1½ T oil to wok. Add black bean mixture and break apart, cooking for a few seconds.
6. Add melon slices, sugar, salt and soup stock. Cover wok, bring to a boil and cook 2 minutes.
7. Add beef to wok, thicken with cornstarch and water mixture to form a sauce.

●

Chicken or prawns may be substituted for the beef, omitting the soy sauce.

Asparagus may be substituted for the bitter melon. Snap off tough ends, rinse asparagus and cut into ½ inch thick diagonal slices about 3 inches long.

CHINESE TURNIP WITH BEEF
(4 servings)

1 lb	Chinese turnips
¼ lb	beef, sliced thin against the grain
1 t	soy sauce
½ t	sugar
1 t	cornstarch
2 T	oil
1	clove garlic, minced
1 T	oyster sauce
½ t	salt
½ C	soup stock
	cornstarch and water for thickening if desired
2	green onions cut in 1 inch pieces

1. Peel turnip and slice into ¼ inch thick diagonal slices. Cut slices into 4 inch long slivers about ¼ inch thick.
2. Combine beef with soy sauce, sugar and cornstarch. Set aside.
3. Heat wok, add 1 T oil and stir fry the beef until done. Remove and set aside.
4. Add 1 T oil to the wok and fry garlic. Add the slivered turnip and stir fry for ½ minute.
5. Add oyster sauce, salt and soup stock. Cover, bring to a boil and cook 5 minutes.
6. Add beef to wok, thicken with cornstarch and water mixture. Garnish with green onions.

●

Cut turnip into larger pieces and cook with red bean curd instead of oyster sauce. Increase soup stock and cook until tender.

PORK AND SHRIMP STUFFED MUSHROOMS
(4-6 servings)

1½ lb fresh mushrooms (24 medium)

Filling Ingredients

½ lb	lean ground pork
¼ lb	fresh prawns (shelled, deveined, rinsed and chopped)
4	water chestnuts, chopped
2 T	chopped bamboo shoots
1 t	minced ginger root (optional)
1 t	soy sauce
1 t	rice wine
½ t	salt
¼ t	white pepper
1 T	cornstarch
1 T	oil
1 T	mirin or sherry
1 T	oyster sauce
2 t	soy sauce
½ C	soup stock
	cornstarch and water for thickening
1	green onion, chopped

1. Wash and dry the mushrooms. Gently break off stems and reserve for another use.

2. Combine all filling ingredients. Stuff mushrooms, dividing filling equally. Use about 1½ teaspoons for each mushroom.

3. Heat a skillet and add oil. Lightly brown mushrooms, meat side down over medium heat. Turn mushrooms over and cook tops for about one minute.

4. Add mirin, oyster sauce, soy sauce and soup stock. Cover, bring to a boil and simmer for about 10 minutes.

5. Thicken with cornstarch and water mixture. Add green onions.

●

Mushrooms may be stuffed ahead and refrigerated.
Use smaller mushrooms and serve as an appetizer.

BEAN THREADS WITH
BEAN SPROUTS AND PORK
(4 servings)

1	3.85 oz. package of bean threads (saifun)
2 T	oil
½ lb	pork, sliced thin
1	small onion, sliced
1	small carrot
2	medium forest mushrooms
¼ C	slivered bamboo shoots
1 lb	bean sprouts
1 C	chicken stock
¼ C	soy sauce
½ t	salt
2	green onions cut into 1 ½ inch slivers

1. Soak bean threads until soft, about ½ hour in warm water; take out and cut into shorter lengths. Set aside.
2. Soak mushrooms until soft, rinse and slice very thin.
3. Peel carrot, cut into thin diagonal slices, then into slivers to resemble bean sprouts.
4. Heat wok, add oil and cook pork on high heat until done, about 2-3 minutes.
5. Add onions, carrots, mushrooms, bamboo shoots and bean sprouts. Reduce temperature and stir fry for ½ minute.
6. Add chicken stock, soy sauce and salt. Add bean threads.
7. Mix all ingredients together and continue to cook until most of liquid is absorbed.
8. Add green onion just before serving.

●

Add 2 teaspoons of hot bean paste for a more spicy taste.
Other meats or vegetables may be substituted.

BEAN SPROUTS WITH PORK
(4 servings)

2 T	oil
½ lb	pork, sliced thin
1 t	soy sauce
1 t	minced ginger root
2 t	cornstarch
1 lb	bean sprouts
1 t	salt
1 T	rice wine or soup stock
2	green onions, chopped

1. Combine pork slices with soy sauce, ginger and cornstarch.
2. Heat wok, add oil and stir fry the pork until done (2-3 minutes).
3. Add bean sprouts, salt and rice wine. Cook 2 minutes.
4. Toss green onions on top.

●

Ground pork may be used instead of sliced pork.

Add some slivered carrots for added color.

This recipe is very good used as a filling for Mandarin pancakes.

PRAWNS WITH VEGETABLES AND MUSHROOMS
(4 servings)

3 T	oil
½ lb	prawns (shelled, deveined, rinsed and cut in half lengthwise)
1	small onion, wedged
2	large forest mushrooms (soaked, rinsed and sliced)
1 C	sliced fresh mushrooms
1	small green pepper, wedged
1	small carrot, sliced thin diagonally
¼ C	sliced bamboo shoots
¼ C	sliced water chestnuts
½ t	salt or to taste
1 T	rice wine
½ C	soup stock
2 t	cornstarch dissolved in 2 T water

1. Heat wok, add 2 T oil. Stir fry prawns for 2 minutes or until done. Remove and set aside.
2. Add 1 T oil to the wok and stir fry all vegetables, adding the salt. rice wine and soup stock.
3. Cover, bring to a boil and cook ½ minute.
4. Add prawns to the vegetables, thicken with cornstarch mixture and stir to combine all ingredients.

●

Substitute prawns with chicken, beef or pork sliced thin.
Other vegetables may be used.

CHINESE BROCCOLI WITH OYSTER SAUCE
(4 servings)

1 ½ lb	Chinese broccoli
¼ C	oyster sauce
2 T	oil
1	clove garlic, crushed

1. Wash broccoli and cut off tough stems.

2. Bring some water to a boil in a large pot.

3. Cook broccoli for 1 minute. Remove and drain.

4. Straighten broccoli, squeeze out excess water and cut in 3 inch sections, discarding uneven stems. Place on a serving dish.

5. Pour oyster sauce over broccoli.

6. Heat 2 T oil in the wok and fry the garlic. Pour hot oil over broccoli and serve.

●

Other green vegetables may be substituted. Cook vegetables in boiling water until crisp tender.

BROCCOLI WITH MUSHROOMS
(4 servings)

2 T	oil
1 lb	broccoli
¼ lb	fresh mushrooms
¾ C	soup stock
1 t	salt

1. Rinse broccoli and mushrooms.

2. Cut broccoli flowerets into 2 inch lengths, separating into small clusters. Peel stem and cut into ½ inch thick diagonal slices.

3. Slice mushrooms into ¼ inch thick slices.

4. Heat wok and add oil. Stir fry broccoli for one minute on high heat.

5. Add mushrooms, soup stock and salt. Cover and cook 4 minutes on high heat. Serve hot.

●

Asparagus can be substituted for the broccoli. Break off tough ends and discard. Cut into 3 inch lengths.

PEA PODS WITH WATER CHESTNUTS
(4 servings)

2 T	oil
1 lb	fresh pea pods
½ C	sliced water chestnuts
½ t	salt
1 T	soy sauce

1. String pea pods, rinse and drain.
2. Heat wok, add oil and stir fry pea pods and water chestnuts for ½ minute.
3. Add salt and soy sauce. Cook another minute or until pea pods are crisp tender.

STIR FRIED CABBAGE WITH CARROTS
(4 servings)

1 T	oil
1	small head of cabbage
1	medium carrot, peeled
½ t	salt
⅓ C	soup stock

1. Cut cabbage into quarters and slice into ½ inch slices.
2. Cut carrot in half lengthwise and slice into thin diagonal strips.
3. Heat wok and add oil. Add cabbage, carrots, salt and soup stock.
4. Stir together all ingredients, cover and cook 1-2 minutes or until tender.

●

This is a very basic stir fried vegetable dish, good for any leafy vegetable such as nappa.

Ham can be substituted for the carrots.

STIR FRIED SPINACH
(4 servings)

2 T	sesame seed oil
2	bunches of fresh spinach
1	clove garlic, minced
1 T	soy sauce
½ t	sugar
2 T	toasted sesame seeds

1. Wash spinach and cut into 3 pieces, discarding stems.
2. Heat wok and add oil. Toss in garlic and allow to fry for a few seconds.
3. Add spinach, soy sauce, sugar and mix well. Cook until spinach wilts.
4. Toss sesame seeds on top and remove to a serving dish.

•

Any leafy vegetable can be used. Try this recipe with lettuce leaves.

SPINACH SHELLFISH SALAD
(4 servings)

2	bunches fresh tender spinach
1 C	cooked shellfish such as crabmeat, prawns, scallops

Dressing

⅓ C	rice vinegar	2 T	sugar
2 T	soy sauce	1 T	mirin

1. Wash spinach thoroughly, retaining stems. Do not cut leaves apart.
2. Place spinach in a pot of boiling water; cook just until wilted.
3. Remove spinach and immediately place into cold water to cool.
4. Hold each spinach plant by the stem, dip in and out of cold water to straighten the leaves. Gently squeeze out water.
5. Cut off stems; cut leaves into 2 inch lengths.
6. Pour dressing over spinach leaves just before serving.
7. Garnish with shellfish.

•

Try this recipe with broccoli flowerets, asparagus or green beans cut into 2 inch lengths. Adjust cooking time for each vegetable. Cook until tender but retain bright green color.

GREEN BEANS WITH FERMENTED BEAN CURD
(4 servings)

1 lb	fresh green beans
1 T	oil
1 T	fermented bean curd (fu yu)
¼ t	salt
½ t	sugar
¾ C	soup stock or water

1. Break off ends of beans and remove strings. Cut beans into 2 inch lengths. Rinse and drain.
2. Heat wok and add oil. Stir fry beans on high heat for about ½ minute.
3. Add fu yu, salt and sugar. Stir together.
4. Add soup stock, cover, bring to a boil and cook 5 minutes or until tender. Be careful not to boil dry. Reduce temperature if necessary.

●

Frozen or canned green beans may be used.

BEAN SPROUT SALAD
(4 servings)

1 lb	fresh bean sprouts
1	green onion chopped

Dressing

3 T	rice vinegar
2 T	sugar
½ t	salt
1 t	sesame seed oil
¼ t	white pepper

1. Bring a pot of water to a boil. Add bean sprouts and cook for ½ minute.
2. Remove from boiling water and rinse in cold water. Drain well.
3. Chill bean sprouts before serving.
4. Combine with dressing and garnish with green onions just before serving.

PORK WITH SCRAMBLED EGGS
(Mu shu pork)
(4 servings)

1 T	oil
3	eggs
½ t	salt
2 T	oil
½ lb	boneless pork, sliced thin
½ C	sliced forest mushrooms
½ C	tiger lily buds
¼ C	cloud ears
½ C	bamboo shoots, sliced
2 T	mirin
dash	soy sauce
¼ C	soup stock
2	green onions, chopped
1	head lettuce

Separate the head of lettuce, using small leaves as cups, and place on a platter.

1. Soak mushrooms, tiger lily buds, and cloud ears until soft (10 minutes). Wash well and slice thin. Set aside.
2. Beat eggs, adding salt. Fry in 1 T oil in the wok to make scrambled eggs and set aside.
3. Add 2 T oil to wok and cook pork on high heat 2 or 3 minutes.
4. Add mushrooms, tiger lily buds, cloud ears, bamboo shoots, mirin and soy sauce. Stir together, adding soup stock, cover, bring to boil and cook 1 minute.
5. Add green onions and mix in eggs, breaking into small pieces.
6. Serve with lettuce cups, steamed white rice or Mandarin pancakes.

●

For a spicy taste, add 1 t of hot bean paste.

CHICKEN WITH SCRAMBLED EGGS
(4 servings)

1	chicken breast, boned and sliced thin against the grain
2 t	soy sauce
2 t	cornstarch
½ t	sugar
1 t	minced ginger root
4 T	oil
3	eggs, beaten with a dash of salt
½ C	shredded bamboo shoots
2	large forest mushrooms (soaked, rinsed, sliced thin)
¼ C	dried cloud ears (soaked, rinsed and chopped)
1 T	soy sauce
1 T	rice wine
2 T	soup stock
½ t	salt
2 t	sesame seed oil
1 t	hot bean paste (optional)
¼ C	chopped green onions
1	recipe of Mandarin pancakes

1. Coat sliced chicken with soy sauce, cornstarch, sugar and minced ginger. Set aside for ½ hour.
2. Heat wok, add 2 T of the oil and cook eggs as in making scrambled eggs. Remove and set aside.
3. Add 2 more T oil to the wok and stir fry the chicken on medium high heat for approximately 4 minutes or until done.
4. Add bamboo shoots, mushrooms, cloud ears, soy sauce, wine. soup stock, salt, sesame seed oil and hot bean paste. Stir fry for 2 minutes, lowering temperature if necessary.
5. Return scrambled eggs to the wok and break into small pieces. Toss in green onions. Mix all ingredients together.
6. Serve with Mandarin pancakes. Place a small amount of filling on the pancake, roll and fold up one end to keep filling from falling out while eating. Lettuce leaves resembling small cups may be served instead of pancakes.

●

Allow guests to roll their own pancakes.
This dish keeps warm very well.

EGG FU YUNG
(4 servings)

½ C	cooked meat (chicken, pork, shrimp, or crab)
½ C	bamboo shoots
½ C	onions
1	stalk celery (½ cup)
1 C	bean sprouts
3	large eggs
1 t	salt
¼ C	oil for frying

Chopped green onions and toasted sesame seeds for garnish

Gravy

1¼ C	cold soup stock
2 T	cornstarch
1 T	mirin
1 T	soy sauce

Bring gravy to a full boil, stirring constantly, just before serving.

1. Chop meat, bamboo shoots, onions and celery. Add the bean sprouts. Do not chop the bean sprouts.
2. Beat eggs with the salt and add to the filling ingredients just before frying.
3. Heat an electric skillet or frying pan to 375°. Pour in the ¼ C oil.
4. Ladle mixture into pan to form small patties. Fry about 2 minutes, turn over and fry 3 minutes more. Adjust temperature as needed (6-8 patties).
5. Wipe pan clean and repeat process, using more oil as needed, until all patties are fried.
6. Serve with hot gravy. Garnish with chopped green onions and toasted sesame seeds.

●

Patties may be made ahead and reheated in the oven. Place on cookie sheet and bake at 375° for 5 minutes.

SHRIMP MUSHROOM EGG FU YUNG
(4 servings)

3   large eggs
        oil for frying (375°)

Filling

½ C	cooked shrimp
½ C	chopped onions
½ C	chopped celery
¼ C	chopped fresh mushrooms
1 C	bean sprouts
½ t	salt

Gravy

1 ¼ C	soup stock
2 t	soy sauce
2 t	mirin
2 T	cornstarch
¼ C	green peas

1. Combine filling ingredients with eggs and mix thoroughly just before frying.

2. Heat an electric skillet to 375° with ⅛ inch of oil.

3. Ladle mixture into pan to form small patties. Fry about 2 minutes, turn over and fry 3 minutes more. Adjust temperature as needed.

4. Bring gravy to a boil, stirring constantly, and serve over patties.

CRAB EGG FU YUNG
(4 servings)

1 C	cooked crab or shrimp meat
1 T	oil
⅓ C	sliced onions
½ C	sliced fresh mushrooms
½ C	chopped chives or other green vegetable thinly sliced
6	eggs
1 t	salt
2-3 T	oil

1. Heat 1 T oil in the wok and stir fry onions, mushrooms and chives just until limp (about 1 minute). Set aside.

2. Combine the crab meat, vegetable mixture, eggs and salt. Beat together.

3. Heat a skillet and add 2-3 T of oil to coat the bottom of the skillet. Add all of the egg mixture and cook in the same manner as scrambled eggs. Cook mixture about 2 minutes.

●

Other cooked meats may be used such as chicken or ham.

SPICY BEAN CURD WITH GROUND PORK
(4 servings)

1	16 oz. cube of bean curd
1 T	oil
1	clove garlic, minced
½ C	ground pork
2 t	hot bean paste (or to taste)
1 T	soy sauce
¼ t	salt
¾ C	soup stock
	cornstarch and water for thickening
1	green onion, chopped
1 t	sesame seed oil

1. Cut bean curd into ½ inch cubes. Set aside.
2. Heat wok, add oil, garlic and ground pork. Stir fry pork on high heat until done (2 minutes).
3. Add hot bean paste, soy sauce, salt, soup stock and bean curd. Cover, bring to a boil and cook gently for 2 minutes.
4. Thicken with cornstarch mixture to desired thickness. Add green onions and sesame seed oil. Mix gently to combine all ingredients.

●

To give the bean curd a firmer texture, cut bean curd into one inch cubes. Fry cubes in an oiled non-stick frying pan to lightly brown all sides. Continue with recipe beginning with step 2.

MUSHROOMS WITH BEAN CURD
(Moo Goo Tofu)
(4 servings)

1 T	sesame seed oil
4	forest mushrooms
1	small onion
½ C	green vegetable
3 T	oyster sauce
½ t	salt
½ C	soup stock
1	12 oz. pkg. tofu (bean curd)
2 t	cornstarch dissolved in 1 T water

1. Soak forest mushrooms in hot water until soft, rinse, and dice in ½ inch cubes.
2. Dice onions and green vegetables such as pea pods or green beans.
3. Cut tofu into one inch cubes.
4. Heat sesame seed oil in a wok until hot, add mushrooms, onions, and green vegetables. Stir fry 1 minute on high heat.
5. Add oyster sauce, salt and soup stock.
6. Add tofu, bring to a boil and cook until hot, being careful not to break tofu apart.
7. Add cornstarch mixture and gently stir until thickened.
8. Serve hot with white rice.

●

Tofu is another word for bean curd.

DEEP FRIED STUFFED BEAN CURD
(4 servings)

Filling (combine all ingredients)

⅓ C	ground pork
⅓ C	chopped prawns (shelled, deveined)
1 T	chopped water chestnuts
1	forest mushroom chopped (soaked and rinsed)
¼ t	salt
1 t	rice wine
1 t	soy sauce
1 t	sesame seed oil
1 T	cornstarch

1	16 oz. cube of bean curd

3 C	oil (350°)

1 T	oil
1	clove garlic, minced

2	forest mushrooms (soaked, rinsed and sliced)
¼ t	salt
1 T	soy sauce or oyster sauce
1 t	rice wine
1 C	soup stock

3 C	lettuce or celery cabbage, sliced
1	green onion, chopped
1 t	sesame seed oil

cornstarch and water for thickening

1. Cut the one pound cube of bean curd into 4 equal pieces.
2. Cut each piece diagonally in half, forming a triangle.
3. With a sharp knife, gently remove some of the bean curd, forming a pocket in each triangle.
4. Carefully stuff each triangle with about 1 T of filling.
5. Heat 3 C oil in the wok to 350°. Deep fry several triangles at a time until light brown (5 minutes), turning once. Remove and set aside. Repeat with the other pieces.
6. Heat a clean wok or frying pan; add 1 T oil and fry garlic for a few seconds.
7. Add mushrooms, salt, soy sauce, wine, soup stock and stuffed triangles. Cover, bring to a boil, reduce temperature and simmer for 5 minutes.
8. Turn temperature up to high, add lettuce and cook until wilted.
9. Add green onions and sesame seed oil. Thicken with cornstarch and water. To serve: Place lettuce on bottom of dish and triangles on top.

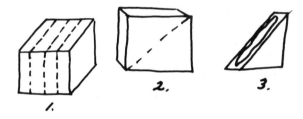

●

The filling is delicious made with a white fish meat instead of pork or prawns.

Other vegetables such as carrots and broccoli may be added with the mushrooms. Slice carrots thin and cut broccoli into flowerets. (omit lettuce)

GLOSSARY

Anise, star — Brown, star shaped seed with the taste of licorice. Used as a spice for sauces. Keeps indefinitely on shelf.

Bamboo shoot — Cream colored, cone shaped shoots of bamboo. Canned shoots are most common. Once opened, store covered with fresh water up to 2 weeks in the refrigerator. Change water once every 4 to 5 days.

Bean curd, fermented (fu yu) — Fermented white bean curd with a cheesy flavor. It is sold bottled in half inch thick squares. Keeps in refrigerator indefinitely after opening.

Bean curd, fresh (tofu) — Usually square shaped, creamy textured, bland curd made from soybeans. Also comes deep-fried and canned. Fresh bean curd, covered with water, can be kept in the refrigerator for approximately one week. Remove from original package and replace with fresh water as soon as possible. Change water every 2 days to keep fresh.

Bean curd, red (nam yu) — Sometimes called wet bean curd. Red soft cubes of fermented bean curd with a strong cheesy flavor. Comes in cans. Once opened, store in jars with a tight lid in the refrigerator indefinitely.

Bean filling, sweet — Thick, sweet bean paste made from beans and sugar. Often used as a filling for pastries. Usually sold in cans. Store tightly covered in refrigerator or freezer indefinitely.

Bean sauce, brown or yellow — Sauce made from soybeans and salt. Often comes in cans. Some bean sauces may contain bean halves and others may be a smooth sauce, similar to Japanese red miso, which can be used as a substitute in some recipes. Keeps indefinitely in the refrigerator in a tightly sealed jar.

Bean threads (saifun or cellophane noodles) — Thin, long, dry noodles made of mung bean flour. Keeps on shelf indefinitely. Soak in warm water for 15 minutes before use. May also be deep fried in hot oil. Do not soak in water if used for deep frying. Use as a noodle in soups or with stir fried vegetables and meats. To keep clean up to a minimum, place noodles in a large paper bag before removing wrapper. Break off amount needed and store remainder in bag.

Bean paste, hot (chili paste with soybean) — Soybean sauce made from soybeans, chili peppers and sometimes garlic. Comes in cans or jars. Refrigerated, keeps indefinitely in tightly sealed jars. Degree of hotness may vary between different brands. Brown soybean sauce combined with a hot sauce can be used as a substitute.

Bean sprouts — Sprouts of the mung bean; about 2 inches long. Refrigerate sprouts covered with water. Keeps for one week. Change the water every 3 days.

Bitter melon — Long, green, pear-shaped melon with a ridged surface. It has a definite bitter taste. Cut melon in half lengthwise and remove seeds. Cut in thin slices and stir fry with meats.

Black beans, fermented — Salted, fermented, soft black bean seed. Mainly used to flavor sauces. Rinse with water before using. Keeps in a covered container on the shelf indefinitely.

Bok choy (Chinese cabbage or greens) — Dark green leafy vegetable with a white stalk. Keeps in refrigerator for one week. High in vitamins A and C.

Broccoli, Chinese — A tender, green, seasonal vegetable available in spring and summer months. Chinese broccoli is more slender and leafy than regular broccoli. For recipes in this book, substitute with bok choy, spinach or regular broccoli cut into long slender pieces.

Cleaver — The knife used to do most all cutting in Chinese cooking. Usually a lighter, thinner cleaver is used for slicing and chopping meats and vegetables. The heavier cleaver is used to cut through bone.

Cloud ears — Brown, irregular, leafy shaped fungus or mushroom with a delicate taste. Soak 15 minutes in warm water to soften. Rinse before using. Keeps indefinitely on shelf when dried. Also called tree ears.

Five spice — Blend of five ground spices; Szechuan peppercorns, star anise, cinnamon, fennel and cloves. Keeps on shelf for several months.

Ginger root — Irregular bulb root of the ginger plant. Hot and spicy in taste. Slice ginger and freeze separated slices. Keeps in the freezer indefinitely. Peel ginger and store in rice wine. Slice and use as needed.

Hairy melon (jit gwa) — Oval shaped, green melon with a hairy surface. Peel, slice thin and use in soup.

Hoisin sauce — Pungent, sweet condiment sauce made of soybeans, spices, chili and sugar. Once opened, store in a jar with tight lid. Keeps refrigerated for about 6 months.

Jelly fish — Body of the jelly fish cut into shreds. Usually sold salted and packaged in plastic bags in the refrigerator section. Store in refrigerator or freezer. Rinse off salt and soak in cold water before using.

Litchi nuts — A sweet, white fruit about 1 inch in diameter. It has a dark red hull which must be removed before eating. Also comes canned and dried. Use as a garnish or as a fruit.

Long beans, Chinese — Foot long, thin green beans. When cooked, resemble string beans but have a more delicate flavor. Treat in same manner as regular green beans.

Maifun (rice noodles) — Noodles made from rice flour. Soak until soft in hot water before using. Also, noodles may be deep fried in hot oil. Do not soak before deep frying. To keep clean up to a minimum, place package of noodles in a large paper bag before removing wrapper. Break off amounts as needed. Store remainder in the bag.

Mirin — Japanese sweet rice wine used in cooking to bring out flavor or to add a little sweetness. Not interchangeable with rice wine.

Miso — Fermented bean paste made from soybeans and rice. Used mainly in Japanese cooking. Red or aka miso is saltier and white or shiro miso is milder or sweeter. Red miso is a good substitute for brown bean sauce. Refrigerate miso in sealed containers indefinitely.

Mushroom, dried (forest or black) — Dried black forest mushrooms have a delicate flavor. Can be stored in covered container on the shelf, indefinitely. Must soak in warm water until soft, rinse, discard stem and use in recipe.

Mustard, dried — Pungent powder. When mixed with water, forms sauce which is used as a dip to accompany barbecued pork and other foods. Store dry powder on shelf indefinitely. Mix 1 tablespoon water to 1 tablespoon dry powder for average proportion.

Osyter sauce — Thick brown sauce made from oysters and soy sauce. Used to enhance flavor or as a dip. Keeps indefinitely in the refrigerator.

Panko (dehydrated bread crumbs) — Japanese dehydrated bread crumbs with a coarser texture than regular bread crumbs. Available at most supermarkets or oriental groceries. To make panko, use white bread and make coarse crumbs in the blender. Then dry crumbs slightly in the oven.

Parsley, Chinese (coriander or cilantro) — A leafy parsley with a pungent flavor. Use as a garnish. Also may be used to add flavor to most any dish.

Sausage, Chinese (lop cheong) — Cured pork sausages about 6 inches in length with a sweet flavor. Refrigerate up to one month or freeze up to several months.

Seaweed, dried — Dried seaweed is usually available in sheets. Keeps indefinitely on the shelf. Some seaweed sheets are more expensive because they are roasted and seasoned. These are used in Japanese cooking.

Sesame seed oil — Golden brown oil of sesame seeds. Buy in small quantities and keep refrigerated after opening. Add to dishes just before serving.

Shrimp, dried — Dried tiny shrimp. Soak in warm water for about ½ hour to soften before use. Keeps on shelf indefinitely in covered jars.

Snow peas (Chinese pea pods) — Flat edible pea pod. Has a delicate taste and comes fresh or frozen. Must string as in green beans before cooking.

Soy sauce — The extract of fermented soybeans combined with salt. Soy sauces range from light to dark. Light soy sauce is the most delicate, and is used as a dip or in cooking; gives little color. Some dark soy sauce has caramel added for color and is slightly sweet. Japanese soy sauce is in the middle and serves most purposes very well. For most recipes, Kikkoman soy sauce may be used unless specified differently in recipe.

Stir fry — To toss, cook or saute in English, chow in Chinese. Slices of vegetables, meats, or a combination are cooked quickly in the wok with a small amount of oil. Liquid may be added to make a sauce and cornstarch is used for thickening. Foods retain more food value, color and texture.

Szechuan vegetable — The knobby bulb of a radish preserved in chili pepper and salt. Rinse before using. Store airtight in jar. Refrigerate indefinitely. No substitutes.

Tiger lily flowers — Dried golden brown tiger lily flowers; about 2 inches long. Soak in warm water about 15 minutes and rinse before use. Keeps indefinitely on shelf when dry.

Turnip, Chinese (lo bok or daikon) — Crisp large white root vegetable resembling a large carrot. Peel skin and slice or shred before cooking. Store in the refrigerator.

Vinegar, rice — A mild vinegar made from rice. Used in most oriental dishes. Keeps indefinitely on the shelf.

Water chestnuts — Walnut sized, brown bulb. Must be peeled before use. It is sweet and has a crisp texture similar to apples. Canned water chestnuts are peeled and boiled. They will keep covered with fresh water, in the refrigerator, for about 2 weeks. Change the water once a week.

Wine lees — A thick fermented wine paste. Light miso (Japanese soybean paste) can be used as a substitute.

Wine, Shaohsing or rice — Chinese rice wine used for drinking or cooking. Dry sherry may be used as a substitute in cooking.

Winter melon (tung gwa) — A large light green melon with a white powdery surface resembling a watermelon. The inside is white with seeds in the center. Usually sold in sections. Peel hard skin and discard seeds. Slice melon and use in soups.

Wok — The wok is a metal pan with sloping sides and a rounded or flat bottom. The 14 inch wok is the best size for home use. Refer to wok in the information section of this book.

Won tons — Fresh squares of noodle dough. Usually comes in one pound packages. Thickness varies from thick to thin. Fresh won tons will keep in the refrigerator one week. Can be frozen, wrapped air tight, for about 2 months. Use thick wrappers for deep fried won tons. Thin wrappers are better for soups.

Legend

t = teaspoon
T = tablespoon
C = cup

The typeface used throughout this book is **Friz Quadrata** medium and bold weights. Recipe titles were set in 14 point Friz Quadrata Bold caps; ingredients and instructions in 9 point Friz Quadrata medium upper and lower case; and notes in 8 point Friz Quadrata medium upper and lower case. Korinna typeface was used for fractions.

INDEX